THE ALI FILES

HIS FIGHTS, HIS FOES, HIS FEES, HIS FEATS, HIS FATE.

NORMAN GILLER

pitch

A Norman Giller Books publication

In association with Pitch Publishing

First published by Pitch Publishing, 2015

Pitch Publishing

A2 Yeoman Gate

Yeoman Way

Durrington

BN13 3QZ

www.pitchpublishing.co.uk

A CIP catalogue record is available for this book
from the British Library.

ISBN 978 178531-014-0

Typesetting and origination by Pitch Publishing

Printed and bound by
CPI Group (UK) Ltd, Croydon, CR0 4YY

Contents

Dedication

Remembering with love, respect and affection my old boxing pals and gurus Terry Lawless, Reg Gutteridge, George Whiting, Angelo Dundee, Terry Spinks, my *Boxing News* editor Tim Riley, stats wizard Ron Olver, promoter czars Jack Solomons and Harry Levene, master matchmaker Mickey Duff and the one and only Sir Henry Cooper.

And with thanks to Muhammad Ali for the memories. Simply The Greatest.

Author's Acknowledgements

MUHAMMAD Ali did the fighting all on his own, but I could not have done the writing without a lot of help in my corner. I have named all the eyewitnesses in the book who willingly shared their observations on the greatest heavyweight fighter ever to climb into the ring, but there has been a lot of unheralded work in the background, particularly from Pitch Publishing pistons Paul Camillin and Jane Camillin, diligent editor Gareth Davis, jacket designer Duncan Olner, proof reader Dean Rockett, and lay-out master Graham Hales.

There are dozens of exceptional ringside reporters whose accounts of the Ali adventure have helped me put together the complete picture of his career, and I am indebted to my old *Boxing News* alma mater for factual checks and to BoxRec.com for its mindblowing online records collection. For our photographs, we bow the knee to the premier photographic agency, PA Photos. Most of all, thanks to my son, Michael Giller, who listened and learned when I was telling him all those bedtime stories of the great champions, and grew up to become a sports statistician who is a reliable safety net for all my facts and figures.

Oh yes, and thanks to Muhammad Ali. Simply The Greatest.

Seconds Out: Norman Giller

THIS book is for all Aliphiles. It is more than 30 years since Muhammad Ali last threw a punch, yet he remains unquestionably the best-known sportsman of all time. There is a generation growing up who only know the legend of Ali, never saw him fight and yet are in awe of him and his fantastic fistic feats. Here in *The Ali Files*, I will give the facts behind the fable.

I was lucky enough to work as a publicist with Ali on some of his European fights, and got to know him as a friend as well as a fighter. In my corner to help me tell the story of The Greatest I have gathered many eyewitnesses of the Ali career – opponents, referees, his trainers, sparring partners, celebrity fans and ringside reporters, who were there as observers of his astonishing adventures in and out of the ring.

As a reporter for the trade paper *Boxing News* in the late 1950s I was aware before most people outside the United States that in Louisville, Kentucky, the descendant of a slave – Cassius Marcellus Clay – was emerging as an exceptional amateur boxer. He won the gold medal in the 1960 Rome Olympics to launch a career that saw him transcend the world of boxing to become, arguably, the most famous and feted man on the planet – and also with some, the most reviled of sportsmen.

The Muhammad Ali I got to know was a softly-spoken, modest gentleman, who became an actor of Olivier class if a microphone or camera came into range. He would switch to the public Ali, loudly, brashly selling seats and making life easy for headline-hunting, deadline-chasing newspapermen and interviewers. He was a born publicist, yet away from the camera was quiet and respectful, and with a mind hungry for knowledge.

Sadly, he got caught up in the poison of politics and what some would describe as the blind bigotry of religion. But, 50 years on from taking the world title from the 'big, bad bear' Sonny Liston, Ali was a contented man as he battled ill health with the same bravery and resilience he used to show in the ring when he was justifiably known as, simply, 'The Greatest'.

I have chosen Ali as the subject for the 99th book with which I have stupefied the great reading public because he is the most dynamic personality I have met in my 55-plus years scratching a living as a sportswriter. I have been lucky to have been in the company of many of the finest sports champions of post-war times, and Ali stands head and shoulders above them all as the most interesting and entertaining.

Millions of words have been written about the ringmaster but few books have given total concentration to each of his 61 professional contests. On the following pages I intend to give an accurate account of each of those fights that turned him into a sporting legend. And to give the book a fascinating twist I reveal what has happened to each of Ali's opponents since they took on The Greatest. You will be surprised, often shocked, by some of the revelations.

In the 1990s I worked with leading television sports producer Neil Duncanson on a TV series commissioned by C4. It was called *Crown of Thorns* and was a history of world heavyweight champions, from John L. Sullivan through to the then title-holder Evander Holyfield. We had just got the Muhammad Ali interviews and data into our file when the series was cancelled following a death in the ring. The project survived only in book form. Now, as a special tribute to The Greatest, I can share with you the facts and figures we could not reveal to the viewers. Here, fight by fight, are *The Ali Files*.

Seconds out…come out writing.

Tunney Hunsaker (USA)

Venue: Freedom Hall, Louisville
29 October 1960
Clay 192lb, Hunsaker 186lb
Clay WPTS6
(Clay purse: $2,000)

C ASSIUS MARCELLUS CLAY, grandson of a slave, was 'owned' by a syndicate of 11 wealthy Kentucky businessmen when he climbed into the ring for his professional debut. Waiting in the opposite corner, experienced but limited Tunney Hunsaker, a 30-year-old journeyman who, away from boxing, was a West Virginian police chief.

Clay was covered in blood at the end of his first fight in the paid ranks – his opponent's blood. Outclassed Hunsaker, pounded for six one-sided rounds by the fleet-footed Cassius, was bleeding profusely from his nose and a cut over his left eye. The 6,180 spectators sensed they were in on the start of something special as their local hero showed off with quick combination punches that continually rocked Hunsaker back on his heels.

Judge Sid Baer scored the fight 30-24 in Clay's favour, judge Walter Beck had it 30-23, and referee Paul Matchuny marked it as a runaway 30-19 for the Kentucky kid. At the suggestion of Clay, proceeds from the fight went to the local Kosair hospital for disabled children. Just 55 days earlier he had written his name into Olympic history by winning the gold medal in the light-heavyweight division in the Rome Games. They were the Olympics that Ali pleaded to miss!

He was petrified of flying, and asked the selectors to leave him out of the team after he had won back-to-back national Golden Gloves titles and the Olympic trials. The 18-year-old Clay, born in Louisville, Kentucky, on 17 January 1942, was finally persuaded to get aboard the Rome-bound plane, but only on the understanding he could wear a parachute. Here was early evidence that the brash young man who talked such a good fight was – in Monty Python lingo – 'something completely different'.

Once on terra firma, Clay proved himself a larger than life character in the Olympic Village and he shook hands with so many fellow competitors before and after his contests that he was nicknamed 'The Mayor'.

Clay was in huge demand by professional promoters after an amateur career in which he won 100 of 108 bouts. He was already showing signs of bitterness after being refused service in a whites-only restaurant, and he claimed he threw his Olympic gold medal into the Ohio River in protest. Many years later his faithful photographer Howard Bingham, who knew him better than anybody, told me, 'That was nonsense. The champ made it up just to show his disgust at his treatment. The truth is he lost his medal and he was given a replacement after lighting the flame at the 1996 Olympics in Atlanta.'

The syndicate of millionaire moguls – the Louisville Sponsoring Group – paid Clay an up-front $18,000 to box under their banner, and dictated that he should join the training camp run by former world light-heavyweight boxing master Archie Moore. But Cassius did not feel comfortable under Moore's tutelage – particularly when he ordered him to sweep the gym floor – and he took off for Miami, where he asked hugely experienced trainer Angelo Dundee to look after him. It was the start of a 21-year partnership.

CLAY AFTER-FIGHT QUOTE, 'That was the heaviest I've ever been in the ring, so I wasn't quite as fast as usual, but I was still too quick for Hunsaker. He could not live with me. I took one good body shot that made me catch my breath, but it was the only time he connected with any punch of note. I found it comfortable going six rounds, and am happy to step up to ten rounds as soon as the promoters want it. There's a lot for me to learn, but I'm confident I'll be in a challenging position for the world title before I'm 21.'

EYEWITNESS – TUNNEY HUNSAKER, 'Clay is incredibly good for an 18-year-old, and I'll be amazed if he doesn't go all the way. You don't win an Olympic gold medal unless you have something special. He didn't hurt me, but he's like lightning and I couldn't stop all the leather coming my way. There are still some amateurish things about him and he's living dangerously holding his hands so low. But I look forward to watching his progress and can always say I was first to fight him as a pro.'

WHATEVER HAPPENED TO TUNNEY HUNSAKER? Two years after fighting Clay, Hunsaker was rushed to hospital with a brain injury following a knockout defeat. He was in a coma for nine days and never fully recovered. He passed on in 2005 aged 74, suffering from Alzheimer's. A Sunday school teacher and the youngest ever local police chief at 27, he was much admired in his home state and there is a Tunney Hunsaker Bridge named in his honour in West Virginia.

Herb Siler (USA)

**Venue: Miami Beach
27 December 1960
Clay 193lb, Siler 191lb
Clay WRSF4
(Clay purse: $200)**

THIS was Clay's first contest with Angelo Dundee in his corner, and he did everything to order on a bill topped by Dundee's future world light-heavyweight champion Willie Pastrano. He sparred dozens of rounds with Pastrano and learned the art of not getting hit from one of the finest ever exponents of defensive boxing.

Herb Siler, the fighter selected as Clay's second opponent, was as much a novice at professional boxing as the Olympic champion. Seven years older, he had come late into the fight game and was having his third contest when he climbed into the ring to face the hottest young prospect in the world.

Born in Alabama, Siler was based in Miami and he was less than pleased when the posters for the fight went up showing him billed as Herb Silver.

By the time the scheduled eight round fight was halfway through he was so dazed and disoriented that he hardly knew his own name.

Nicknamed 'Bowlegs' because of his cowboy-style stance, Siler tried to take the fight to Clay but found himself hitting thin air as the Louisville fighter revealed the flashy footwork that would become such an important part of his armoury.

Siler was out of his depth, and continually had his head knocked back by Clay's fast fists and it was quickly obvious the fight would not go the distance. A series of left jabs and then a follow-through right cross had Siler hanging on in the third round, and the bell saved him from further punishment as an over-enthusiastic Clay went all out for a stoppage. Nobody could question Siler's bravery and determination, but he was up against a phenomenally talented opponent who oozed confidence and class.

As the one-way traffic continued, the referee came to Siler's rescue in the fourth round after a fusillade of combination punches from long range had sent him reeling against the ropes.

Clay showered quickly so that he could be at ringside to watch his new friend and guru Pastrano, who in the top-of-the-bill contest lost a world title eliminator on points to Jesse Bowdry. It was a huge form shock and taught the young Clay that nothing could ever be taken for granted in boxing.

CLAY AFTER-FIGHT QUOTE, 'I was astonished that Willie got beaten. Having sparred with him, I was convinced he would be too clever for Bowdry. I have learned lots of defensive tricks from him. He is a master. It was a real eye-opener for me when he lost, and now I know that professional boxing is going to take every ounce of my concentration if I'm gonna meet my goals. Siler gave me no trouble at all, but he's had less ring experience than me so I just did what was expected of me. It was great having Angelo Dundee in my corner. He is such a wise man, who knows all the tricks of the trade – the king of trainers, and I'm going to become the king of heavyweights.'

EYEWITNESS – ANGELO DUNDEE, 'Cassius and I are getting on famously. He sure can jaw, but he is an intelligent young man who also knows when it's right to listen. We have got each other's respect. He is a quick learner and we will soon iron out the few faults he has brought with him from the amateurs. His feet are as fast as his fists, and we need to get him to plant his feet for when he throws his big bombs.

'Yes, he can be cocky, arrogant even, but it's no use being a shrinking violet in this business. He could do with a few more pounds on that great frame of his, and we are working on that. I've been around the fight trade for a few years now and I have not seen a better heavyweight prospect. My job is to make sure he reaches his potential. He has the talent, he has the hunger and he has the ammunition. Watch this space.'

WHATEVER HAPPENED TO HERB SILER? After retiring from the ring following a 27-fight career in which he won 15 contests, Siler's life went into a nosedive. He was sent to prison for seven years on a manslaughter charge in 1972 after shooting a girlfriend. Blaming alcoholism for his problems, he found God while he was locked up and became a sober, devout Christian. He was running his own construction business when he died in 1985 aged 66. His grandson, Brandon Siler, was a top NFL linebacker.

Tony Esperti (USA)

**Venue: Miami Beach
17 January 1961
Clay 195lb, Esperti 197lb
Clay WRSF3
(Clay purse: $545)**

CASSIUS celebrated his 19th birthday with an impressive third-round destruction of an opponent who was listed in the record books as retired. Tony Esperti, originally based in Brooklyn and now relocated to Florida, had not fought for five years apart from as a sparring partner in the Miami gyms. Known as 'Big Tony' and notorious for openly mixing with mobsters, most of his professional boxing career – dating back to the early 1950s – had been more about taking part than winning.

According to the boxing record books, Esperti was born in 1932. But the more reliable police records showed 1930. An idea of his vintage is that when he had his second professional fight at Madison Square Garden the legendary Joe Louis was topping the bill!

Esperti had sparred with top fighters of the quality of Sonny Liston and Willie Pastrano, but he was not in the same league as Clay, who showed off the moves he and Angelo Dundee had been working on in training. There was a new authority to his punches, and ring-rusty Esperti was continually forced to hold on as the leather ripped through his defences.

It got to the point in the second round where Clay started to toy with his outmatched opponent, and in the interval he got a telling-off from Dundee for clowning.

Suitably admonished, Clay put his foot on the accelerator in the third round, and a sustained two-fisted attack had the giant 6ft 3in Esperti all at sea and referee Mike Kaplan jumped in to stop it, much to the annoyance of the ringside spectators who thought he had been premature with his decision.

Clay hardly broke sweat, and as his arm was raised in victory he looked resplendent in the white USA shorts he had worn when winning the gold medal in Rome. Esperti on the other hand, looked as if he had been put through a bacon slicer. He had only one more fight before retiring to concentrate on criminal activities that were to end in tragedy.

CLAY AFTER-FIGHT QUOTE, 'I gave myself a birthday present against an opponent who was dangerous but did not really belong in the same ring as me. Heavyweights around the world are gonna start losing sleep as they realise this new kid on the block means business. I'm Olympic champion. Now I have my sights set on becoming the champion of the whole world.'

EYEWITNESS – REFEREE MIKE KAPLAN, 'Some spectators booed because they thought I stopped it too quickly, but they didn't have the up-close view that I had. Clay was busting Esperti up with every punch and his eyes were in a mess and he was out on his feet. I had no doubts I'd got it just right when I stepped in. It was my opinion he had taken enough punishment against a kid who is as exciting a prospect as any young fighter I've ever seen. His fists are like lightning, and I've never known a heavyweight move so fast around the ring. This kid is something very special and will make the boxing world buzz. What's more, he knows it!'

TONY ESPERTI

WHATEVER HAPPENED TO TONY ESPERTI? Esperti could not escape his past as a mobster, and in 1967 he was sentenced to life in prison for the cold-blooded murder of a gangland boss. It remains one of the most infamous crimes in Miami's violent history, and it went down in the annals as the Halloween Night Murder. Blown up to 250 pounds and really looking the part of his 'Big Tony' nickname, he walked into an all-night bar in Miami and fired five bullets from a revolver into feared Mafia leader Tommy 'The Enforcer' Altamura.

Witnesses were reluctant to come forward because of threats, and it took two trials and a hung jury before Esperti was finally found guilty. It was reckoned that the hardest fight of his life was in the police station when he was charged with the murder. It took six officers to overpower him in a bloody brawl. Esperti had been arrested 11 times previously, but he slipped through the police net every time because witnesses suddenly seemed to lose their memories. He died on 12 April 2002, aged 72.

Jim Robinson (USA)

**Venue: Miami Beach
7 February 1961
Clay 193lb, Robinson 178lb
Clay WKO1
(Clay purse: $645)**

J IM ROBINSON did not belong on the same planet, let alone in the same ring as the lean and hungry Cassius. The man from Miami via Kansas was brought in as a last-minute substitute by desperate promoter Chris Dundee (Angelo's brother) after original opponent Willie Gulatt had gone missing.

A week before the fight Clay had sparred with Swedish heavyweight hero Ingemar Johansson, who was preparing for his third world title showdown with Floyd Patterson. Clay seized the publicity platform to announce himself as 'the future champion of the world.' He danced rings around the ponderous-looking Swede, shouting for all to hear, 'Look at me, look at me, I'm dancin' with Johansson.' He made it rhyme, a sign of things to come. Johansson's management took offence at Clay's showboating and refused to let the Swede complete the scheduled six rounds of sparring.

Rumours flew that former basketball professional Gulatt had seen Clay making a fool of Johansson and that he skipped town rather than face the young upstart. Gulatt preferred the story that he had declined because his purse money was not sufficient to warrant being a stepping stone for the hottest property in town. Chris Dundee searched high and low for a new opponent, and went very low to Jim Robinson, a blown-up middleweight. His weight was given as 178lb, but he later insisted he was closer to 158.

He had given himself the nickname 'Sweet Jimmy', but his ring record suggests more sourness with only eight victories decorating his 33 fights. The quickest of his defeats came against Clay. He lasted just 94 seconds. Clay's fists were a blur as six punches crashed through Robinson's apology of a defence, and he folded to the canvas. He was gamely on his feet at 'nine' but the referee continued the count and ruled it a first-round knockout.

It was embarrassing all round, because everybody knew Robinson should never have been in the ring with Clay. The *Miami News* ringside reporter wrote scathingly, 'If promoter Chris Dundee had canvassed the women in the audience, he couldn't have found an easier opponent for Clay.'

It did not stop Clay strutting around the ring as if he had beaten a world-rated opponent. He was still pumped up from the publicity he had earned following his sparring session with Johansson.

CLAY AFTER-FIGHT QUOTE, 'I can only beat what's put in front of me. I got the job done nice and quick, and put Robinson out of his misery. Now I can't wait to get it on with whichever opponent they come up with next. There's nobody gonna be able to live with me. Ask Ingemar Johansson. He now knows I'm the quickest and the most dangerous heavyweight fighter in the universe. I should be fighting Fraud Patterson for the world title, not him.'

EYEWITNESS – PROMOTER CHRIS DUNDEE, 'Jim Robinson did us a favour taking the fight at short notice. He would not have been our choice, but we were let down at the last minute. Cassius Clay is the man that many bought their ticket to see and we did not want to let them down. He is a phenomenal prospect, and the hardest thing will be finding opponents brave enough to get into the ring with him.'

WHATEVER HAPPENED TO JIM ROBINSON? That's a good question! He seemed to disappear off the face of the earth after finishing his career with 17 defeats in his last 18 fights. Wright Thompson, an outstanding sportswriter with ESPN, spent six fruitless years trying to trace Robinson's whereabouts, basing his 'Shadow Boxing' series of articles on his search for Clay's fourth opponent. His obsession was triggered by Aliphile Stephen Singer, a New Hampshire car salesman who gave himself the target of collecting the autographs of the 54 men who climbed into the ring with Clay/Ali. He got 53 to sign. The only one who eluded him was Jim Robinson. As I write, Robinson's fate after his retirement from the ring remains a mystery. His 94 seconds of fame was defeat by The Greatest.

Donnie Fleeman (USA)

Venue: Miami Beach
21 February 1961
Clay 190lb, Fleeman 184lb
Clay Won RET6
(Clay purse: $913)

MINDFUL of the criticism they got for putting Clay in with the undistinguished Jim Robinson, the Dundee brothers chose to go a big step up in class for his fifth fight. In the opposite corner 45-fight veteran Donnie Fleeman, a tough Texan who had won 34 contests and drawn one. He had been 'strictly an opponent' against top-ranked fighters of the class of Sonny Liston and Roy Harris, and had a great but flattering scalp when beating over-the-top ex-world champion Ezzard Charles.

Former farm boy Fleeman claimed once getting so angry with a stubborn mule that he knocked it out with a huge right swing. But what could he do with a floating butterfly with the sting of a bee?

Topping the bill for the first time, the international spotlight was now on Clay as he started to attract media attention with outrageous statements, many of them borrowed from a professional showman/wrestler modestly calling himself Gorgeous George. 'Gaseous Cassius' bought himself a pink Cadillac, and introduced himself to complete strangers in the street as 'a future heavyweight champion of the world'.

Fleeman joined in the ticket-selling hype and promised to 'put this young pup in his place'. But the young pup proved more of a grown Rottweiler and gave the Texan such a bad mauling that immediately after the fight he announced his retirement from the ring.

This was comfortably Clay's most complete performance to date. He dazzled Fleeman with his speed of foot and fist, and the 29-year-old former Golden Gloves champion hardly landed a punch as his young opponent peppered him non-stop with combination punches delivered from long range.

The fight was scheduled for eight rounds, but from halfway through the referee was looking anxiously at Fleeman, who was almost being hit at will. The punch that once knocked out a mule would now have had trouble flattening a gnat as Fleeman tried to retreat from the painful punishment, but Clay was showing him no mercy as he chased him around the ring.

For Fleeman, admired for his resistance and having been stopped only once, there was no hiding place.

At the end of the sixth round the Texan held up his hands in surrender, complaining of a broken rib. More like a broken heart.

The crowd gave Clay a standing ovation. He was beginning to attract a following of fans who shared his opinion of himself.

His next fight was due on the undercard of the Patterson–Johansson world championship decider, but a bruised hand meant he had to pull out.

CLAY AFTER-FIGHT QUOTE, 'I admit I was scared thinking about this fight. Fleeman has been in the ring with the best in the business, and anybody who can go twenty rounds with Roy Harris and beat Ezzard Charles has to be taken seriously. But look at me. Not a mark on me. I didn't let him lay a glove on me. I made HIM look like the novice. Only trouble I had was bruising my knuckles because I hit him so many times.'

DONNIE FLEEMAN

EYEWITNESS - DONNIE FLEEMAN, 'That's it for me. I took a big beating in there tonight, and it's convinced me it's time to get out. This kid is unbelievably fast. He treated me like a punch ball and I just couldn't get out of the way. I felt like a sitting duck and took it as long as I could until my ribs felt as if they were being hit with bullets. They were hurting like hell and I just couldn't go on. I took one heck of a hiding. That's enough. I shall watch Clay with interest. He's got all the ammunition, that's for sure. Just wish I could have given him a better fight, but the rib damage was just too painful.'

WHATEVER HAPPENED TO DONNIE FLEEMAN? True to his word, Fleeman never fought again. He hung up his gloves and became a machine operator at Proctor & Gamble. Donnie was a popular, amusing, loyal man who served his country in the US Air Force, and was happily married for 50 years. But he later paid the price for having too many fights and taking too many punches. His final years were lost in the fog of dementia and he had no memory of his career when he died in Red Oak, Texas. He was 81.

LaMar Clark (USA)

Venue: Louisville
19 April 1961
Clay 192lb, Clark 181lb
Clay WKO2
(Clay purse: $2,548)

THE Louisville Sponsoring Group running the Clay show decided the time was right for the local hero to return to Kentucky, but they were concerned when trainer Angelo Dundee proposed LaMar Clark as his sixth opponent. They were worried by an impressive Clark ring record that showed a world record 44 successive knockout victories. Was this the sort of fighter against whom Clay should be risked while still learning his trade?

This was the question Group chairman Bill Faversham put to Angelo, who knew the form of fighters inside out. He was able to put the chairman's mind at rest by pointing out that 40 of those victories had been against novice fighters, many having their first contests. Of his 49 fights he had lost the only two times he came up against experienced professionals, including 1956 Olympic heavyweight gold medallist Pete Rademacher.

Standing 5ft 10in and weighing 181lb, Clark was out of Cedar City, Utah, a born brawler who used often to have as many as five fights a night in local halls when building up his reputation as the knockout king. His record was six in one night, all won by knockout. He sometimes took on wrestlers, and always beat them with his punching power, but boxing aficionados knew that under Queensberry rules his freedom to punch would be controlled by strict refereeing.

LaMar was a chicken farmer when he was not fighting, but was never chicken in the ring and he was convinced he could become cock of the walk against Clay, who for the first time predicted the round in which he would win. 'Clark will fall in two,' he told the media before the fight.

The tactics Clark chose were tailor-made for Clay, who stood off and picked his punches as LaMar came charging at him without lateral movement and his head held invitingly high. It almost finished in the first round when Ali sent Clark staggering back against the ropes with a jolting right hand to the jaw. The man from Utah was under pressure and soaking up punishment when the bell came to his rescue.

Midway through the second round Clay unleashed his finest punch combination to date, four rapid left hooks followed by a sweeping right cross that sent Clark tumbling on to his side for the full ten-second count.

The final punch broke Clark's nose. The millions watching on national television were impressed by the 'Kid from Kentucky', who was now being referred to as the 'Louisville Lip' because of his constant chattering before, during and after his fights.

CLAY AFTER-FIGHT QUOTE, 'What did I tell you? Round two. He's been knocking over a load of bums, and had no chance of beating a class fighter like me. I enjoyed winning in front of my hometown folk. Go and take a picture of the house where I was born. That will be a shrine one day. They'll be coming from all around the world to see the place where Cassius Marcellus Clay was born.'

EYEWITNESS - ANGELO DUNDEE, 'It took me a week of hard talking to get Bill Faversham and his business partners to accept

Clark as an opponent. I worked harder than Cass did in the ring. They were really worried by his record, but you have to look at the quality of the opposition. He had beaten a bunch of nobodies. Well now he's met a real somebody and look what happened. I've worked with hundreds of fighters, but I've never been as excited as I am by this kid. He talks a good fight...he fights an even better one.'

WHATEVER HAPPENED TO LAMAR CLARK? Like Donnie Fleeman, Clark announced his retirement immediately after his crushing defeat by Clay. He was only 27 and made the wise decision that he did not want to get hurt again. He returned to his chicken farm, and turned his back on boxing. Later, this Korean War veteran worked for the Kennecott Copper mine company in Utah while he and his wife of 46 years raised three daughters. He was a proud and faithful teaching member of the Mormon Church right up until his death at the age of 72 on 5 November 2006.

Duke Sabedong (USA)

**Venue: Las Vegas
26 June 1961
Clay 194lb, Sabedong 225lb
Clay WPTS10
(Clay purse: $1,500)**

THIS was Clay's first ten-round fight, his first in the 'boxing capital' Las Vegas and the first where he switched on the full publicity gusher. He had been so impressed by the shouting and boasting of wrestler Gorgeous George that he decided to turn up the volume and roar the most outrageous things that came to mind. 'I am the prettiest,' he would say at every interview. 'This Duke Sabedong is too ugly to share the ring with me. I'm going to box his ears off. I'm gonna knock him all the way back to Hawaii, and he won't need a plane.'

Sabedong, nicknamed Kolo, was a 30-year-old giant who stood 6ft 6in and weighed more than 16st in old money. To prepare Clay for the fight Angelo Dundee brought in a huge sparring partner who was building a towering reputation for himself. This was Ernie Terrell, who would play a large part in Clay's future.

A former Waikiki beach boy, Sabedong had won 15 of 28 fights since turning professional in 1954 and was noted for his immense strength and stamina rather than his boxing skill. He had been in the ring with opponents of the class of Zora Folley, Carl 'The Truth' Williams and Howard King.

There was a stark contrast in styles from the moment of the first bell, when Clay set off like a greyhound out of the traps while Sabedong was more like a plodding carthorse. Clay was a thoroughbred in comparison as he literally boxed rings around Sabedong, catching him repeatedly with accurate left jabs and overarm rights before retreating out of range as his opponent attempted telegraphed counter punches.

Clay was already proving himself a chatterboxer, holding conversations with ringside spectators and shouting in derision at the outclassed Hawaiian. Between rounds Angelo Dundee continually had to remind him to concentrate on his fighting. Already he was dividing the opinions of fans, some who loved his style and confidence, others who thought he was a young braggart who needed a lesson. He was not going to get it from the totally outpunched Hawaiian.

In frustration, Sabedong cut up rough and hit Clay low several times, and then got two points deducted for landing a heavy, swinging blow long after the referee had shouted for them to break.

Clay gave the sad-looking Sabedong a boxing lesson and was a unanimous winner at the end of ten hectic rounds. Referee Harold Krause scored it 50-34, judge John Romero 50-38 and judge Dick Kanellis 49-43, all for the Louisville Lip.

As the cocky Clay acknowledged the applause of the spectators, he kept shouting, 'You're looking at the future heavyweight champion of the world…the w-h-o-l-e world.'

Years later, the man from Louisville told me, 'I used to watch a blond-haired wrestler called Gorgeous George combing his hair in the ring, and telling the world how pretty he was and that his opponents were too ugly to be allowed to fight him. He got everybody riled up, and then I'd look around the arena and not an empty seat to be seen. Man, I thought, that's what I'll do. I'll use my mouth as well as my fists to get myself noticed. I owe Gorgeous George a lot.'

Clay was introduced to a New York-born comedy writer called Gary Belkin, who helped him polish the poems with which he started entertaining the world and undermining the confidence of his opponents. Cassius was like a pioneer rapper, and it was Belkin – scriptwriter for huge comedy stars like Sid Caesar, Carol Burnett and Danny Kaye – who gave rhyme and rhythm to his verse. He deserves to be mentioned in any record of the life and times of Clay/Ali.

CLAY AFTER-FIGHT QUOTE, 'Look at me, ten rounds of fighting a monster and I don't have a mark on me. I'm even prettier than when I started. The only time he caught me was when the referee had told us to break. That was very sneaky, but it's a lesson I have to learn about professional boxing. Defend yourself at all times. I hope Fraud Patterson was watching. I'm after his title.'

EYEWITNESS – DUKE SABEDONG, 'The kid is good. No doubt about it. But he needs to shut his mouth. Boxing is about what you do with your fists, not your tongue. He was disrespectful. I've been in the ring with much heavier punchers but nobody to match him for speed. It's going to take somebody special to beat him. But he's not unbeatable, like he thinks. Nobody is.'

WHATEVER HAPPENED TO DUKE SABEDONG? He retired in 1964 after a first-round knockout defeat by former world title contender Eddie Machen. His final record was 36 fights, won 17, lost 16, drew two, one no decision. He returned home to Hawaii, became a popular tour guide and also worked as a corrections centre officer. Duke and his wife, Maureen, had a huge family, including eight grandchildren and five great-grandchildren. He died in Hilo Medical Center – just a mile from where he had been born – in 2008. Duke was 78.

Alonzo Johnson (USA)

Venue: Louisville, Kentucky
22 July 1961
Clay 188lb, Johnson 210lb
Clay WPTS10
(Clay purse: $6,636)

FOR the first time, Clay's young ears were assaulted by boos and jeers when – in his toughest test to date – he looked sluggish and lacking aggression and ambition against ring-wise Alonzo Johnson. He was paying the price for his pre-fight boasting, but he responded to the demands of trainer Angelo Dundee and stepped up his work rate in the last third of the fight to take complete command.

There were scandalous accusations, persisting to this day on the internet, that the three scoring officials – referee Don Asbury and two judges – were paid to score the fight for Clay. It was nationally televised and film of the fight exists to prove beyond reasonable doubt that he won comfortably.

He had called Johnson the 'old man' before the contest in front of his hometown fans, but his opponent was still months short of his 27th birthday. In experience terms, compared with Clay, this former barber was a ring veteran. Born in Mississippi but fighting out of Pennsylvania, he had won 19 of his 26 fights, including victories over high-ranking Nino Valdes, Jimmy Slade and Willie Pastrano.

Clay boxed on the retreat for much of the first half of the fight, and his negative tactics irritated many of the ringside spectators who wanted to see him put action to go with his well-publicised predictions of a stoppage victory.

Dundee had to work hard in the corner to motivate strangely lethargic Clay, who finally came to life in the last two rounds. Johnson had battled to the edge of exhaustion, and was clinging on in desperation as his young opponent put on the pressure with a series of two-fisted attacks that had him rocking and rolling around the ring.

There was a mixed reception as the MC announced the three scorecards: Referee Asbury 50-44, judge Warwick Edwards 48-45 and judge Walter Beck 48-47, giving Clay a unanimous points victory.

Johnson, half an inch under six feet and really a blown-up light-heavyweight, had told the media in the week before the fight that he had a secret weapon, 'I sparred with the kid earlier this year and know how to beat him. I've got a surprise for him. But I'm keeping it to myself. You'll see in the ring in Louisville. I'm goin' to humiliate him in front of his hometown fans. It's time he was shut up, and I'm the man to do it.'

CLAY AFTER-FIGHT QUOTE, 'Man, I've never been so hot in my life. You could have fried an egg on the canvas under those television lights. I thought I was going to melt away. But I conserved my strength for that grandstand finish. Johnson's had much more experience than me, but he could not stay the pace, and I had him in all sorts of trouble in those last two rounds. I showed I have stamina, atomic energy and determination to go with my unequalled skill. I said before the fight that I would systematically eliminate Johnson. And that's exactly what I did, slowly chipped away at him until he had no resistance left. Guess we'll never know what his secret weapon was.'

EYEWITNESS - ALONZO JOHNSON, 'The kid can talk all he likes, he just ain't got it. He didn't hurt me once. I don't know what fight the referee was watching. He was in there with us, saw it right in front of his nose. How could be give the kid every round? I thought I sure as hell had done enough to take it. I'm the victim of a hometown decision. But Clay's the money ticket. No way they were going to let me spoil the party.'

WHATEVER HAPPENED TO ALONZO JOHNSON? Following his defeat by Clay, Johnson had 15 more fights of which he won just four. In the summer of 1963 he travelled to London to act as a Clay impersonator while sparring with Henry Cooper before the Englishman's first fight with the Louisville Lip. Alonzo hung up his gloves in 1972, finishing with a ten-round points win over Henry Culpepper in Tokyo. Topping the bill was Muhammad Ali, defending his world title against Mac Foster. Johnson made the trip as Ali's chief sparring partner. He retired to Pennsylvania, and is the great uncle of American footballer Demetrius Baldwin-Youngblood.

Alex Miteff (Argentina)

**Venue: Louisville, Kentucky
7 October 1961
Clay 188lb, Miteff 210lb
Clay WRSF6
(Clay purse: $5,645)**

ANNOYED by the press criticism that followed his victory over Alonzo Johnson, Clay came out with all guns blazing at the start of his ninth contest against Argentina's bull of a fighter, Alex Miteff. He wanted to prove that his attacking armoury matched that of his defensive skills, but he was facing an opponent who soaked up punishment like blotting paper.

Born in Santa Fe in 1935, Miteff had been a market worker since he was seven and developed brawn rather than brains. He became an outstanding amateur, winning 126 of 140 bouts. When he turned pro in 1955 he was quickly persuaded to hunt his fortune in America, and he moved to New York where he became an instant favourite at the old St Nicks Arena and Madison Square Garden.

Standing 6ft 1in and weighing just over 200lb, he had an aggressive style and was noted for his wicked body punches. He won his first 12 fights in the States and was talked of as a future world title contender, but by the time he took on Clay he had become disillusioned after a manager had ripped him off and he had nine defeats denting his 35-fight record. He had breathed new life into his career by joining the stable of highly rated coach Gil Clancy, and knew that a victory over the up-and-coming Clay would put him back in the ratings.

Miteff walked into an early hurricane against Clay and did well to survive the onslaught before giving as good as he got by getting to close quarters and working away to the body. For a change, Clay was anchoring his feet and concentrated on making each punch count.

When it was clear that the Argentine iron man was not in the mood to submit to the pressure, Clay followed Angelo Dundee's orders to 'get back to your boxing'. Just as it looked as if the Kid from Kentucky had settled for a points victory he suddenly caught Miteff with a thundering right cross to the point of the jaw midway through the sixth round.

The Argentine folded slowly to the canvas like a puppet that had had its strings cut, and when he got to his feet with the count coming up to seven he went walkabout in zombie fashion, completely out on his feet. As Clay moved forward to complete the destruction, referee Don Asbury had no option but to wave the fight over as he led the bemused Miteff back to his corner.

Miteff came into the ring wearing a pair of trunks he had borrowed from Clay. He may have had the emperor's clothes, but not his skill.

CLAY AFTER-FIGHT QUOTE, 'Those critics who have tried to hang the "Cautious Clay" label on me had better think again. That punch that finished the fight would have knocked over a horse. I showed tonight I can fight as well as box. I have all the tools, and know when to produce them. Miteff is a brave man and most would have folded long before he did. But even this famous hard man could not stand up to my finishing punch. I am still on course to be the youngest ever world heavyweight champion. Are you listening, Fraud Patterson?'

ALEX MITEFF

EYEWITNESS – GIL CLANCY, 'We had a plan to come on strong in the later rounds, but there were no later rounds. It was an impressive finishing punch by Clay, but there's still a lot of work for Angelo Dundee to do. He is an impressive athlete, no doubt about that, but he's still got much to learn about his craft. There's still a whiff of the amateur about him. He sure talks a lot. I just hope he remembers to listen.'

WHATEVER HAPPENED TO ALEX MITEFF? Soon after his fight with Clay, Alex – known as Pablo to his pals – got a walk-on part in the famous boxing film *Requiem for a Heavyweight*, that could have been his life story. He is the guy standing at the bar with a plaster over his eye in the opening scene. Miteff had three more fights after his defeat by Clay, making an ill-judged comeback against Jerry Quarry in 1967, when he was knocked out in the second round and convincing him that he should hang up his gloves. He won 25 of his 39 professional fights. Miteff considered going home to Argentina to live but finally settled in New York and ran a van hire and limousine business, driving clients to their meetings. In later life he was admitted to a Manhattan nursing home, telling anybody who would listen, 'Ali was tough, but my wife was tougher!'

Willi Besmanoff (Germany)

Venue: Louisville, Kentucky
29 November 1961
Clay 193lb, Besmanoff 205lb
Clay WRSF7
(Clay purse: $2,048)

A CONCENTRATION CAMP survivor, Willi Besmanoff came to the United States in 1957 to chase his dream of following Max Schmeling as a world heavyweight champion. He had won 37 of 48 fights in Germany, but all that action had taken its toll and he struggled to make his mark across the Atlantic apart from as a journeyman opponent.

He had lost 21 of his 30 fights in America when he took on the fast-rising Clay. By now he was an American citizen and settled in Milwaukee, a long way from his Munich roots where he had grown up in Nazi Germany and been imprisoned in Buchenwald because his father was an American Jew. His mother got his religion changed to Protestant to win his release, and he became a baker's boy while taking up boxing.

Besmanoff was nothing if not brave. He was not the best but fought the best, generally finishing on the losing end. Among the top fighters who beat him were Sonny Liston, Archie Moore, Zora Folley, Willie Pastrano, Eddie Machen and Bob Foster.

He promised to put Clay in his place, convinced that he would be too experienced for the young upstart, who was beginning to annoy more people than he pleased with his bragging. 'Clay has never met anybody as tough as me,' he said during the ticket-selling hype. 'I will wear him down until he is too exhausted to talk anymore. That will please many people.'

But Besmanoff could not put action to go with his words. Clay was simply too fast, too strong and too powerful for him. His fists were almost a blur as he beat a tattoo on the face of the heavy-footed German, who was on the receiving end of a painful pounding from the first bell until the merciful climax in the seventh round.

A bowling alley manager when he was not boxing, Besmanoff was finally skittled after two knockdowns convinced referee Don Asbury that enough was enough. Clay was proving he was not a concussive puncher, but it was the culmination of blows that eventually brought his tough-as-teak opponent to his knees. It was totally one-sided.

Bill King, the man who promoted Clay's hometown fights in Louisville, rated this his most outstanding performance to date. 'Cassius has to be considered a serious challenger for the world title already,' he said. 'There's nobody around who matches his speed and skill. Patterson and Johansson have had the world title to themselves for too long, and they are killing boxing with their monopoly. Now we have a genuine master of his art ready to give the championship the lift it needs.' Clay – surprise, surprise – seconded this opinion.

CLAY AFTER-FIGHT QUOTE, 'Anybody who can't see I am ready to take Fraud Patterson is blind, and anybody who can't hear me coming for Patterson is deaf. My fists are so fast that only those with 20-20 vision can see every punch I throw. Besmanoff was brave, but he shouldn't have been allowed in the same stadium as me let alone the same ring. He certainly didn't see most of my punches. I have the fastest fists in history.'

EYEWITNESS - WILLI BESMANOFF, 'Can't take it away from Clay, he's quick. But he's not the unbeatable fighter he thinks he is. I've been hit much harder. Sonny Liston is a much more brutal puncher. He's the only opponent who has ever frightened me in the ring. An animal, and Clay had better keep away from him. My plan was to beat up his body, but he kept running away and I was too slow to catch up with him. The referee could have let me box on. I still had lots to give.'

WHATEVER HAPPENED TO WILLI BESMANOFF? Like so many fighters who don't know when to get off the mountain, Besmanoff fought on for six more years and 14 more fights, seven of which he won. He finally retired in 1967 following three successive defeats, including back to back wars with an equally tough warrior in George Chuvalo. His first wife walked out on him, and he disowned his father after he had sued him for room and rent. He lived in New York, Atlanta and finally Florida, where he set up a successful bakery business, using the knowledge he had picked up as a baker's boy in Germany. He happily remarried, and had two daughters and two grandchildren. Willi passed on - a veteran of 93 fights - in 2010, aged 78. What a life!

Sonny Banks (USA)

Venue: Madison Square Garden, NY
10 February 1962
Clay 194lb, Banks 191lb
Clay WRSF4
(Clay purse: $5,014)

IF you're ever on *Mastermind* and are asked who was first to floor 'Muhammad Ali/Clay' you will know not to say Henry Cooper, because that distinction was grabbed by Sonny Banks. It happened in Clay's debut in New York, where his boasts and gimmicks had not set the Big Apple alight. There were only 2,000 spectators in the huge, historic Madison Square Garden to see him get off the canvas to win against a hardly distinguished opponent.

Banks, a rangy, 6ft 2in, 21-year-old Ford automobile worker from Detroit, had won ten of his 12 professional fights and had only brief experience as an amateur. He was considered a bright prospect, but not in Clay's class.

As usual, Clay had been telling the world what he was going to do to his opponent, predicting before the national televised fight, 'Banks will come tumbling down in four.'

He opened up at his customary rapid pace, peppering the Michigan fighter's face with a series of fast jabs. It was completely unexpected – particularly by Clay – when, with a minute to go in the first round, Banks came out of a crouch in a neutral corner with a perfectly placed left hook to the jaw. It was delivered as a counter punch from close quarters and startled Clay dropped to the seat of his pants.

Clay was embarrassed as much as hurt and jumped up at the count of two but was forced to take a mandatory eight count from the most famous of all referees, Ruby Goldstein.

A 5/1 betting favourite, Clay quickly regained his composure and had Banks on the retreat at the bell. In his corner, trainer Angelo Dundee told him, 'Hold your right hand up to protect your jaw. All this kid's got is a left hook.'

Round two, and Clay came out with mean intent. He fired a stream of left-right combinations that jolted Banks. Now it was Clay's turn to throw a left hook to the jaw, and it was Banks on his backside. Like Clay, he jumped up at two and had to take the mandatory eight count.

It was all one-way traffic in the third round and Banks was twice sent reeling against the ropes. Referee Goldstein looked set to step in when the bell saved him.

The ringside doctor examined Banks during the interval and advised Goldstein that Banks should not be allowed to take much more punishment. Ruby took note and stopped it after just 26 seconds of the fourth, with Banks still unsteady on his feet after the beating he had taken in the previous round.

CLAY AFTER-FIGHT QUOTE, 'That was embarrassing. I had to give him a good beating for making me look a fool. Once I got up I did what I had to do, and proved I am what I say I am – The Greatest. *Ring Magazine* are rating me number nine in the world. Believe me, there's no way there are eight fighters on this planet better than me. I'm going to have me that world title before I'm 21.'

EYEWITNESS – RUBY GOLDSTEIN, 'I've refereed the best from Louis, Sugar Ray Robinson and just about every great fighter there's been since the 30s, and this kid Clay could one day be up there with them. But he's still got a lot to learn about defence. This game is not only about punching but also avoiding being punched. He had his hands full with Banks, but once he had got over the shock of that knockdown he looked the business. The kid's got heart to go with his ability. That's a big plus. But he must not be reckless. The ring's a dangerous place.'

WHATEVER HAPPENED TO SONNY BANKS? Just three years after his fight with Clay, Banks tragically died following a ninth-round knockout defeat by Leotis Martin in Philadelphia, in May 1965. He slipped into a coma in hospital two days after the contest. An operation to remove a blood clot from the brain was unsuccessful. It was his seventh defeat in 25 fights. When he was told the news, Clay – preparing for his world title defence against Sonny Liston – said, 'Sonny Banks was a fine fighter and a good human being. We earned each other's respect in the hardest arena of them all, the boxing ring. My deepest sympathy goes to his family. This is a hard, hard sport, but we choose to do it knowing the risks. I pray for Sonny's soul and that he rests in peace.'

Don Warner (USA)

**Venue: Miami Beach
28 February 1962
Clay 195lb, Warner 189lb
Clay WRSF4
(Clay purse: $1,675)**

T HE eyes and the ears of the boxing world were now on Clay as he set out to be a fistic prophet and a poet, predicting the rounds in which he would win his fights and often using rhyming lines. For Don Warner, out of the fighting cauldron of Philadelphia and once a hot tip for the top, he came up with the forecast, 'After the fifth round, I warn Warner he'll not be around.'

The publicists went to work for Warner, and he countered, 'I've sparred many rounds with Clay and know exactly the way to beat him. I found his weakness in the gymnasium, and I will expose it in the ring. Obviously I'm not going to tell you what it is, but you'll find out when I shut his big mouth when we meet in Miami.'

Warner had been touted as a future world title contender when he first started out as a professional in 1958, and he lost only one of his first 13 contests. But his star had fallen coming into the fight with Clay following five defeats in his last seven bouts. He saw Clay as a stepping stone back into the limelight.

It was clear they did not like each other when, at the weigh-in, Warner refused to shake Clay's hand and turned his back on the Kentucky showman as he was telling the photographers, 'I am The Greatest. Feel privileged to be photographing this beautiful face.'

The early stages of the scheduled ten-round fight were even until the last moments of the third when Warner appeared to shake Clay with a swinging right to the chin. As he tried to follow up with Clay looking in distress the bell rang.

The Philadelphian convinced himself that Clay would still be suffering from the effects of the punch at the start of the fourth round, and he came charging wildly from his corner. Big mistake. Clay was waiting for him and met Warner with a right, delivered with all his strength straight from the shoulder. He went skidding backwards as if he had been launched and fell through the ropes, on to the ring apron.

Climbing back as the count reached eight, Warner had been parted from his senses and tottered towards Clay, who had his fists cocked for a two-fisted attack as referee Cy Gottfried jumped in to stop the fight at 34 seconds of the round.

Warner complained that he could have fought on, but the referee had saved him from a hiding. He was clearly in a dazed state and Clay was in no mood to show mercy.

CLAY AFTER-FIGHT QUOTE, 'I had predicted round five but I brought it forward because Warner showed me no respect when he refused to shake my hand. I know there are some folk out there who don't like my boasting and shouting my mouth off. But I'm putting the excitement back into boxing. I never say something I don't believe I can do. I want people to come and see me and find out that I'm not all talk. I am The Greatest, I am The Prettiest... I am the next heavyweight champion of the whole world.'

EYEWITNESS - ANGELO DUNDEE, 'As we waited for the bell for round four I told Cassius to prepare himself 'cos I would hear Warner's cornermen telling him my boy was in trouble and that he should get to him quickly. He was wide open as he came rushing across the ring, and Cass met him full on and took him out with a peach of a punch. That straight right almost launched him into space. I reckon in six or so fights' time Cassius will be good and ready to challenge for the world title. I would back him to beat Patterson right now.'

WHATEVER HAPPENED TO DON WARNER? The one-time prospect became a trial horse and finished with a ring record that read: 30 fights, 13 wins (12 inside the distance), 14 losses, three draws. He retired in 1967 after a run of seven successive defeats. Warner came to London in 1963 as one of Clay's sparring partners for his non-title fight with Henry Cooper at Wembley and appeared on the undercard, losing on points over eight rounds against Henry's twin brother, George (billed as Jim). Warner followed the same path as Clay into studying the Muslim religion and retired to Philadelphia with the new name, Hasan Muhammad.

George Logan (USA)

Venue: Los Angeles
23 April 1962
Clay 196lb, Logan 205lb
Clay WRSF4
(Clay purse: $9,206)

THE old 'Brown Bomber' Joe Louis was the figurehead matchmaker for Clay's first fight in California, and closed circuit television guaranteed him his biggest purse to date. Providing the opposition was a potato farmer called George Logan, the 'Boise Bomber' from Idaho, a 30-fight veteran who at his peak had once climbed as high as the fifth-ranked heavyweight in the world.

Louis invited Jack Dempsey to watch Clay sparring in the week before the fight, and the two legendary champions agreed he was an exceptional talent. 'I would have fancied my chances to knock him out because of the way he holds his hands low,' said the 'Manassa Mauler' Dempsey. 'But I have to admit he's faster on his feet than anybody I can remember fighting. But he's not as clever as Tunney, and certainly not as powerful as my dear friend Joe Louis. I'm convinced he'll become world champion some time soon.'

George Logan, idolised back home in Idaho, was a gentleman, and Clay found it difficult to whip up hatred against a man he respected. So he made himself the talking point. He worked tirelessly selling the fight, walking around the streets of Los Angeles and introducing himself to complete strangers. 'Hi, I'm the greatest fighter on the planet,' he would say. 'I'm the most exciting thing to hit California since the Gold Rush.'

He entertained TV interviewers with the shouted prediction, 'My Logan Slogan is that he'll fall in four, even if the crowd call for more.'

Starting as a 6/1 favourite, Clay gave Logan a boxing lesson and was hitting him almost at will as he danced around the ring. He clowned and chatted and seemed to be thoroughly enjoying himself as he scored freely from long range, never giving the slow, deliberate Logan the time to plant his feet and score with punches from close range.

By the third round Logan's face was a bloody mess as he suffered cuts over and below his eyes. Even worse was the fact that his nose was busted and he was swallowing his own blood from the second round.

With one minute 34 seconds gone in the fourth referee Lee Grossman and Logan's corner were in unison. The referee moved in to stop the slaughter just as the towel came fluttering in to signal surrender to a Clay in stunning form. It was an easy workout against an opponent whose plodding, walk-forward style was tailor-made for the Kentuckian.

'I'd have done better if my nosebleed had not handicapped me,' said a battered Logan. 'The kid's a great prospect. Can't argue with that, but I wish he'd stop with the talking. This game is about fighting with your fists, not your tongue. But I couldn't shut him up, so I have to admit I lost to a better man.'

CLAY AFTER-FIGHT QUOTE, 'I have been honoured to box for the legend that is Joe Louis, who has always held the title of The Greatest, and I am his natural successor. George Logan was very brave in that ring tonight. Many fighters would have gone down under the pressure I was putting him under. More and more people are now beginning to believe me. I'm going to be the world champion. There's nobody and nothin' that can stop me.'

EYEWITNESS - JOE LOUIS, 'Clay is the hottest prospect for years. He shoots off at the lip, but he gets away with it because he then produces the goods in the ring. Logan is a good puncher but if you can't get near your opponent than you have problems. Clay was just never there to be hit. The kid's like greased lightning. I know what it takes to win the world heavyweight championship, and I think Clay has got it.'

WHATEVER HAPPENED TO GEORGE LOGAN? Fighting on for three more years, Logan took his ring record to 25 wins (16 inside the distance), nine defeats and two draws before starting a new career. He gave up his back-breaking work as a potato farmer and became a police officer in his beloved Boise, and then switched to the truant department, working with youngsters, who hero-worshipped the man many consider the best heavyweight ever to come out of Idaho. George always represented his sport with dignity and dedication.

Billy Daniels (USA)

Venue: St Nicholas Arena, NY
19 May 1962
Clay 196lb, Daniels 189lb
Clay WRSF7
(Clay purse: $6,000)

THIS was billed as 'The Battle of the Unbeaten Warriors'. Like Clay, Billy Daniels had won all his fights – 16 of them – since turning professional at the age of 22 in 1960. 'Somebody's perfect record has gotta go,' Clay trumpeted before the fight. 'But it ain't gonna be mine. I'm gonna take a short cut to victory on TV-live, and the fightin' barber will fall in five.'

Billy's day job was cutting men's hair, and Cassius had a ball making fun of his occupation during the build-up to a contest that came in the middle of a freak heatwave. New York temperatures hit 100 and under the ring and television lights it was like stepping into a sauna.

Born in North Carolina but based in Brooklyn, Daniels first came to prominence when boxing for the US Air Force team, and he then won a New York Golden Gloves title. Daniels was a Big Apple favourite and his St Nicks fan club was convinced he was going to be the man to shut the big mouth of the cocky Kentuckian. His namesake was singer Billy Daniels, who had a huge hit with

'That Old Black Magic'. Boxer Billy promised ring magic against the Louisville Lip.

Clay was an inch and a half shorter than his beanpole opponent, and despite the fierce heat the fight was fought at a fast pace with both men setting out to box at long range. There was an early advantage to Clay when in the second round he opened a gash over the left eye of his lanky rival with what looked to be a chopping right cross, but the Daniels camp insisted it was a clash of heads that caused the damage. From the end of the third round the ringside doctor was a constant visitor to the Daniels corner as his seconds worked at trying to stem the blood seeping from a deep wound.

Desperation started to creep into the Daniels attacking work, and he managed to cause Clay considerable concern with a series of looping right hands to the head. The biased New York crowd jeered Clay at the end of the fifth round after he had failed to meet his pre-fight prediction, but Daniels was slipping behind on the scorecards because of his preoccupation with trying to defend his damaged eye.

Clay now put his foot on the accelerator and was targeting the injury, scoring with double and triple jabs as Daniels dabbed at the flowing blood. Referee Mark Conn was watching with increasing anxiety, and reluctantly halted it at two minutes and 21 seconds of the seventh after a volley of punches had worsened the cut.

The scorecards at the end had Clay comfortably in front, with the referee scoring it five rounds to one, and the two judges agreeing on a four rounds to two advantage. There was not the usual strutting and boasting from Clay as the result was announced, and he showed genuine concern for Daniels and his appalling injury that needed hospital treatment for stitching.

CLAY AFTER-FIGHT QUOTE, 'I can't pretend that I enjoyed that. I like to beat opponents with my skill and speed, not by cutting them. You've gotta believe it, I hate the sight of blood. But I am a true professional and got the job done efficiently and effectively. The barber man was the local boy, but I was a cut above him. He has beaten everybody who has been put in front of him, but he could not stop my march towards the world title. I've provided more evidence that I truly am The Greatest.'

EYEWITNESS – REFEREE MARK CONN, 'I was concerned about the cut from the moment it opened in the second round. I asked the ringside doctor to keep a check on it, and had no option but to stop it when it became a gusher in the seventh. His corner complained that it was a head, but it was clearly a punch that caused the damage. Clay is one helluva prospect, and acted like a true professional in there.'

WHATEVER HAPPENED TO BILLY DANIELS? Following his defeat by Ali, Daniels forced his way back into the picture as a possible world title contender by beating the highly rated Doug Jones when coming in as a last-minute substitute. But his career went into a nosedive after he lost to Cleveland Williams. He retired several times to concentrate on his original career as a barber, but kept getting drawn back to the ring and did not have his final fight until a first-round knockout by Richard Roy in 1977 when he was 40. It was time to return to the less painful business of cutting hair. His final ring record: 49 fights, won 23 (11 inside the distance), lost 22, drew four.

Once his barbershop days were over in Harlem, Billy retired to his home state of North Carolina with his memories of a full life well lived. He said in an interview on the 30th anniversary of his fight with the then Cassius Clay: "I might have got the better of him except for the cut. But that man was so quick he could duck out of the way of my best punches and send them back with his autograph on them!"

Alejandro Lavorante
(Argentina)

Venue: Los Angeles
20 July 1962
Clay 199lb, Lavorante 208lb
Clay WRSF5
(Clay purse: $15,149)

AMBITIOUS Alejandro Lavorante arrived in the United States at the age of 23 in 1959, dreaming of world heavyweight title fame. He stood 6ft 4in, weighed 200 pounds, and gave up his job as chauffeur/bodyguard to deposed Argentine dictator Juan Peron to chase his dream. It was all to end in a tragic nightmare.

Alejandro came from the same Rosario hometown as the revolutionary Che Guevara, and started boxing at school. He became amateur heavyweight champion of Argentina and elected to fight as a professional in the States after Jack Dempsey had spotted him and predicted he could be a future world title challenger. As well as a perfectly chiselled physique, he had film star good looks and featured on the front cover of *The Ring Magazine* as 'a golden prospect' after a stunning seventh-round knockout of top-ranked Zora Folley.

He was chosen as Clay's 15th opponent following a tenth-round demolition by Ageless Archie Moore, and Cassius managed to turn it into a beauty as well as boxing contest. 'How dare this man challenge me not only as as The Greatest but as The Prettiest?' he roared at interviewers as he worked at putting bums on seats for what was his biggest-earning fight to date.

His prophecy, 'The Argentine Man Mountain will come tumbling down in five. Get ready for an avalanche.'

While his bragging was grabbing the headlines, there were plenty of critics dismissing him as what *Sports Illustrated* described as 'more clown than contender.'

But Clay had captured the imagination of the fans and the fight drew a crowd of 11,000 to the Sports Arena, with gate receipts of $64,000. They witnessed an impressive performance from a Clay in the mood to show he was more contender than clown.

Lavorante was outgunned from the first bell, and referee Tommy Hart was close to stopping it in the second round as the South American reeled against the ropes under a two-fisted assault. The bell saved him, but only for more punishment. Clay spent the next two rounds almost playing with his opponent, like a cat with a ball of wool. He was turning it into an exhibition, showing off his fast footwork and even faster fists.

Then, for the predicted final fifth round, he planted his feet and hammered in solid punches that dropped the luckless Lavorante for two long counts before the referee came to his mercy. At the finish he was badly bashed up and would not have won any beauty contests.

CLAY AFTER-FIGHT QUOTE, 'I could have finished it much earlier, but kept it going so that I reached the predicted round. Look at me, I'm even prettier than when the fight started. Now look at Lavorante. Who's the prettier? No question about who's the greater. Now I want Fraud Patterson and the very ugly Liston to sort out their business so that I can get my rightful crack at the title.'

EYEWITNESS - ANGELO DUNDEE, 'Cassius got the balance just right tonight between clowning and delivering the goods. Those experts who are critical of his clowning don't understand the psychological advantage it gives him over opponents. They don't know how to react when he suddenly does something from left field. It throws them and entertains the fans. There has never been a fighter quite like him in the history of boxing. As Al Jolson used to say, "You ain't seen nuttin' yet."'

WHATEVER HAPPENED TO ALEJANDRO LAVORANTE? Just two months after being battered by Clay, Lavorante fought the undistinguished John Riggins and was knocked out in the sixth round, his fifth defeat in his 24 fights. He was taken to hospital and slipped into a coma. His father arranged for him to be brought home to Argentina, where he died 19 months later on 1 April 1964 from the brain damage. He was 27. It should be on the conscience of a lot of people that the gentle giant was allowed to fight Clay so soon after his hammering by Archie Moore and then put into the ring with Riggins. Boxing can be the Ugly Game.

Archie Moore (USA)

Venue: Los Angeles
15 November 1962
Clay 191lb, Moore 204lb
Clay WRSF4
(Clay purse: $45,300)

THE publicity machine went into overdrive with this matching of the two greatest showmen on the sporting scene. Moore had started his career seven years before Clay was born, and had long been a master of talking a good fight. They kicked up a storm before a punch had been thrown to the extent where they sold out the 16,200-capacity LA Sports Arena and had fans queuing to see the fight on closed-circuit television in 53 cities.

Moore – 'Ageless Archie', 'The Old Mongoose' – had briefly trained Clay at the start of his career, and insisted he knew his weaknesses as well as his strengths. 'He has not met anybody near my class,' he said. 'They have fed him a diet of nobodies. Now he's about to meet a real somebody, who has been in with and beaten the best.'

Clay came up with the rhyming prediction, 'Don't block the aisle and don't block the door…You'll all go home after round four.'

Moore, 45 years old and collecting a guaranteed $75,000, responded, 'Only way I'll fall in four is by tripping over Clay's prostrate frame. I've developed a new punch...I call it the Lip-Buttoner, and it's Clay's lip that's goin' to be buttoned.'

But it was old Arch who was knocked speechless by a Clay at his imperious best. New world champion Sonny Liston was among the ringside spectators who saw Moore completely outmanoeuvred and outpowered by his brash and cocky young opponent, who on this night switched from Clown Prince to Crown Prince.

Long-range punches rained through Archie's famous crossed-arms defence as Clay danced and pranced round the creaking old champion. Moore hardly landed a punch as his tormentor gave him the promised boxing lesson, and in the last minute of the third round it looked as if referee Tommy Hart was going to intervene as the old champion took heavy punishment as he sagged on the ropes in Clay's corner.

Somehow Archie managed to last the round, but the inevitable had only been delayed until the fourth – the round that Clay had selected for the *coup de grace*. A long left hook started the final act, Moore sinking slowly to the canvas for the first of three counts. He dragged himself up at eight, but was instantly put down again on to the seat of his pants, his left leg bent painfully under him. Bravely and looking every minute of his 45 years, Moore got up to meet another volley of punches and as he sank for the third time the referee ignored the timekeeper's count and waved it all over and raised Clay's hand.

Clay immediately looked towards world champion Liston and indicated that he was next. 'He won't last long with me,' Sonny told the press. 'He's just a runner and I'd quickly catch up with him.'

CLAY AFTER-FIGHT QUOTE, 'Now everybody's waking up to the fact that I really am The Greatest. The round I call is when they fall. Liston's next.

'I might let him hang around for eight rounds. Archie Moore is acknowledged as one of the all-time greats, but he could not lay a glove on me. How great does that make me? And just look at me, pretty and without a mark on me.'

EYEWITNESS – ARCHIE MOORE, 'The sun's not quite gone down on me, but there's a cloud over me tonight. But there will be new rays of sunshine in the morning, and that's when I'll decide my future. Guess I under-rated Cassius. He's brainier than I thought and boxed a perfect fight. He's brainier than Patterson, who beat me for the world title when a similar age to Cassius. It's early for him to take on Liston. He's got plenty of time. He must show a little patience, and then the title will be his for the taking.'

WHATEVER HAPPENED TO ARCHIE MOORE? Archie had just one more fight after losing to Clay, bowing out following a third-round knockout victory over Mike DiBiase in Arizona on 15 March 1963. His extraordinary record read: Fights 219, wins 185 (including a world record 131 knockouts), 23 losses and ten draws. He stayed in boxing as a trainer, including working with George Foreman for the Rumble in the Jungle. Archie was 81 when he died following a heart attack on 9 December 1998. There will never be another quite like him.

Charlie Powell (USA)

Venue: Pittsburgh
24 January 1963
Clay 205lb, Powell 204lb
Clay WKO3
(Clay purse: $14,331)

CHARLIE POWELL was one of the most talented all-round sportsmen in the United States in the 1950s and 60s. He played basketball for the Harlem Globetrotters, was a top track and field athlete, had a year as a professional baseball player, and became a famed and feared backliner with the San Francisco 49ers. At 19, he was the youngest ever NFL player. But it was in boxing that he made international headlines, knocking out world number two heavyweight Nino Valdes, and eventually earning himself a showdown with Louisville Lip Cassius Clay.

The eldest of nine children – all of them exceptional athletes – Powell stood 6ft 4in, and remains a legend in his hometown of San Diego, where many of his records set while at high school still stand. Clay was well aware of his sporting history, and made a play on it when doing the ticket-selling spiel for the fight, which was being staged in Pittsburgh.

'He is gonna wish he stuck to the other sports,' he said. 'Nobody's getting in for free, but they should know I'm gonna end it in three.'

He added that he would leave the country on the first flight out of Pittsburgh if he lost 'to a dumb American footballer'.

His astonishing run of predictions, with only one wrong to date, had captured the public imagination, many buying tickets in the hope of seeing him get his mouth shut. Powell promised to 'do a Valdes' on him, and they talked the fight up so well that they set an 11,238 record for an indoor fight in Pittsburgh.

Powell decided to try to outgab Clay and kept taunting him from the first bell. 'Come on big mouth,' he challenged. 'Let's see what you're made of.' Meantime, Clay was outjabbing the Californian and hitting him with every punch in his armoury.

It was quickly obvious that Powell had decided to gamble everything on a one-punch finish, while Clay concentrated on hitting and running. A well-placed left hook to the head visibly shook the Kentuckian in the second round, and then a looping right hand to the ribs made him stop in his tracks and gasp for breath. He responded with a fast flurry of punches that had Powell rocking and covering up on the ropes.

Round three was halfway through when Clay suddenly stood his ground and unleashed a volley of punches to Powell's head. He sank to the canvas like a huge liner going down at sea. Referee Ernie Sesto's count had reached eight when he pulled himself to his knees, but he could not get to his feet before ten seconds had been tolled.

CLAY AFTER-FIGHT QUOTE, 'Powell hurt my ribs with one decent shot and there was a left hook that got through, but I was hitting him with twenty punches to his one. I proved yet again that I have become the unbeatable prophet of boxing. I'm working to a timetable, and am on schedule to win the world title in ten months' time. I am the Louisville Lip, and when my lips move they set records. The world is learnin' to listen and learn. What I say goes.'

EYEWITNESS - CHARLIE POWELL, 'I fought the wrong sort of fight against Clay. I should have used my jab more. But I had made up my mind to floor him with one punch. I just wanted to get one shot on that big mouth of his, but he was too quick for me. When he first hit me I said to myself, "I can take two of these to get one in myself." But in a little while I found myself getting dizzier and dizzier every time he hit me. He throws punches so easily that you don't realise how much they hurt you until it's too late He is an outstanding boxer, but needs to be taught a lesson in humility.'

WHATEVER HAPPENED TO CHARLIE POWELL? He had six more fights after facing Clay, hanging up his gloves following a two-round knockout defeat in London by British heavyweight prospect Billy Walker in 1965. His ring record read: 39 fights, 25 wins (17 inside the distance), 11 defeats and three draws. He became a member of the NFL Advisory Board helping retired footballers, and played a vociferous role in knocking down the racist barriers in sport, acting as a spokesman for the National Alliance of African American Athletes. Charlie retired to Pasadena, and celebrated his 80th birthday in 2013. In California he remains revered for having been one of the finest all-round sportsmen of any time, and there was widespread mourning when, suffering from dementia, he passed on in September 2014.

Doug Jones (USA)

Venue: Madison Square Garden, NY
13 March 1963
Clay 202lb, Jones 188lb
Clay WPTS10
(Clay purse: $57,668)

LAY'S carefully planned bragging and boasting was now having the desired effect – putting bums on seats. He was fighting highly regarded New Yorker Doug Jones in his own back yard, and they sold out the 18,732-seater Madison Square Garden for the first time in six years, and this with the New York papers on strike. Huge crowds also gathered at the 40 closed-circuit venues in 38 cities, many of them buying tickets in the hope of seeing the Louisville Lip buttoned.

It was a near-classic contest – voted the Fight of the Year by *Ring Magazine* – but it did not end in the way Clay had loudly prophesied. When the match was first made he had predicted a six-round stoppage, but just before the fight – with a few tickets still left to sell – he went on television to say, 'Jones was going to fall in six, but now I'm cutting his time to four because he has become a disrespectful bore.' With no newspapers to carry his prose, Clay went to a convention of beatnick poets in Greenwich Village and delivered the following:

'Marcellus vanquished Carthage/Cassius laid Caesar low/
And Clay will flatten Doug Jones/With a mighty, muscled
blow! So when the gong rings/And the referee sings out "the
winner" Cassius Marcellus Clay/Will be the noblest Roman
of them all'

Clay, a 3/1 betting favourite, said he was angered by Jones posing
for a picture in which he was reading a book with a mock-up cover
titled, 'The Rise and Fall of Cassius Clay'.

Just before the weigh-in, Clay said to Jones as they posed for
photographs, 'How tall are you, Mr Jones?'

'Why ask that?' Jones replied, warily.

'So's I know in advance how far to step back when you fall in
four,' said Cassius, drawing a roar of laughter from his supporters
and of derision from those who wanted his big mouth shut.

Jones did not fall in four, or six, or at any other time during
their ten-round war. Though he won the decision, Clay was loudly
jeered by the bulk of the audience who considered him flattered
by the points verdict.

Many considered this Clay's least effective performance since he
came on the radar as a possible world title contender, boxing with
unnatural caution after a blockbuster of a right hand had stopped
him in his tracks midway through the first round. He regained his
senses and was in command by the time they reached the fourth
round during which the crowd continually mocked him as he failed
to floor Jones.

Angelo Dundee was concerned to the point that at the end of
the seventh round he shouted in Clay's ear, 'No tomato red for you.
Unless you buck up, you can kiss it goodbye.'

Before the fight Clay had said that as a victory present he would
buy himself a tomato-red Cadillac convertible he had seen in a
showroom. It was a clever psychological trick and Clay stepped
up his work rate in the last three rounds to clinch victory. As they
came out for the final round, Clay said aloud, 'Hello tomato red…
Goodbye Mr Jones.'

The fight looked close to all but referee Joe LoScalzo. Unbelievably, he scored it 8-1-1 to Clay, with the two judges seeing it as 5-4-1. Thirteen of the 25 ringside reporters scored it narrowly for Jones.

World champion Sonny Liston, watching on closed-circuit TV, said, 'If they put Clay in the ring with me I'll get locked up for murder.'

CLAY AFTER-FIGHT QUOTE, 'I exhausted myself selling the fight. How many tickets did Jones sell? He ducked out of that and trained while I was working my butt off making sure people came. I underestimated him, but I still won with lots to spare. Now I want that bum Liston. He'll fall in eight. And I've got a date with a tomato-red Cadillac.'

EYEWITNESS – DOUG JONES, 'I'm not knocking Clay's big mouth 'cos he made me a lot of dough. But he's not the fighter he says he is. It was a close fight and I think I should have got the decision. He should fight me again rather than going near Sonny Liston.'

WHATEVER HAPPENED TO DOUG JONES? Clay and Jones boxed a six-round exhibition in Louisville on 27 October 1966. It was a total humiliation for the New Yorker, who could not lay a glove on the Kentuckian as he danced around the ring jabbin' and gabbin'. The bout was so one-sided it wrecked any hopes Jones had of a rematch. He retired a year later, with the ring record: Fights 41, wins 30 (inside the distance 20), losses 10, drew one. He fought six world title holders and was rated one of the finest fighters never to win a world crown. In 2013, aged 75, he was inducted to the New York State Boxing Hall of Fame.

Henry Cooper (GB)

Venue: Wembley Stadium
18 June 1963
Clay 207lb, Cooper 185lb
Clay WRSF5
(Clay purse: $56,098)

A N unfunny thing happened to Cassius Clay on his way to a world championship challenge against Sonny Liston. Britain's Henry Cooper whacked him on the whiskers with his famed and feared left hook at Wembley Stadium, and for a few dramatic moments it looked as if he had thrown a spanner – or, rather, a hammer – into the works.

The British public didn't like Clay at all when he arrived in London for the fight, shooting his mouth off and shouting things like, 'Any more jive, and Cooper will fall in five.' And he went an insult too far when he called the great English hero 'a bum and a cripple'.

People thought he was getting under Cooper's skin because he and manager Jim Wicks refused to react to his taunts. However, they were on a percentage of ancillary rights, and so the more people who watched on TV or at the cinema the more money they got. Shout away, Clay!

Clay didn't do himself any favours with the crowd when he came swaggering into the ring wearing a huge crown that somebody had found for him in the wardrobes at the London Palladium, where they weighed in with 2,000 people looking on from the theatre seats. He wore the pantomime crown for a laugh, but most spectators thought it was in poor taste and booed him into the ring.

The wily old Wicks had pulled a stroke at the weigh-in. He did not want to give Clay the psychological advantage of knowing that Cooper weighed only 12st 12lb (180lb), and so slipped jockey's handicap weights into his boots so that he added six pounds on the scales.

It was an unforgettable big fight night, full of pomp and ceremony as veteran Jack Solomons called on every trick he had learned in his long career as a promoter who always mixed showbiz with boxing. To call the atmosphere electric would have been an understatement; more like nuclear. Liz Taylor and Richard Burton, the world's most glamorous couple at the time and fresh from making the controversial *Cleopatra* film, were among the 55,000-crowd singing in drizzling rain to the music of the Coldstream Guards band.

Then, heralded by eight trumpeters dressed as if for a coronation, came the two gladiators, picked out in spotlights, Henry from the home dressing room used by England's footballers and Clay approaching from where the visiting teams prepared for action. Ear-splitting cheers for Cooper, just as loud jeers for the cocky Clay, who entered the arena with the golden crown on his head.

The choruses of derision when Clay climbed into the ring were so loud that the ring announcements could hardly be heard. It was sheer bedlam. But the hullabaloo had no effect on the kid from Kentucky as he strutted around the ring as if he owned Wembley.

Henry, eight years older and 26 pounds lighter than his jet-paced opponent, surprised Clay by opening up much more aggressively than in his usual cautious starts to contests, and within a minute referee Tommy Little was warning Clay for holding as

Henry worked to the body like a man possessed. 'Gaseous Cassius' suddenly knew it was not going to be as easy as he had been boasting, and he twice looked appealingly at the referee as Henry roughed him up inside, trying to make the most of his experience as a professional against a relative baby having only his 19th fight.

At the end of a fast and furious first round there was a sign of blood – and it was coming from Clay's nose where the Cooper jab had done the damage.

The second round was even, with Clay now carrying the fight to Cooper and jabbing more effectively. Henry tried hard to drive him back to the ropes, but he was dancing and side-stepping his way out of danger every time the British champion set himself for a two-fisted attack. He was responding to the shouted commands from trainer Dundee, 'Stick and move…stick and move…' In English lingo, that meant jab and move.

All was going to plan for Henry until in the third round he was hit by his old hoodoo – Clay had opened a cut over his left eye with a chopping right hand counter. Suddenly Henry was looking through a veil of blood and there was now desperation in his punches as Clay began toying with him so contemptuously that Bill Faversham – head of the syndicate of businessmen who owned his contract – screamed out, 'Stop clowning, Clay, and get the job done.' He knew that a multi-million dollar title fight with Liston was next on the menu, and Sonny's manager Jack Nilon was there to confirm it.

Jim Wicks wanted to stop the fight at the end of the third round because the gash was so deep, but Henry demanded one more round. And what a round!

It has become etched into fight folklore. But from this distance, let's try to get the facts right and sort the truth from the legend.

Clay continued to clown and box with his hands down at his waist, rolling out of the way of Henry's punches and making him miss with clever ring movement. It was clear – cockily and confidently – he was trying to make the fight last until the fifth round, as he had so noisily predicted. But while he was playing the fool it meant he was not hitting Henry and making the cut worse, and all the time Britain's hero was plotting and planning how he could get home with his hammer.

The round was into its last ten seconds when Clay got himself trapped in a neutral corner as Henry fired a succession of left jabs. They were all rangefinders for the following left hook that landed on an arc flush on the right side of Clay's jaw.

He fell back into the ropes and slithered slowly to the canvas like a melting giant bar of chocolate. The count had reached five and Clay (dropped only once before by Sonny Banks) made the novice decision to get up on legs that were betraying him, but before Henry – acknowledged as one of the best finishers in the business – could move in the bell rang.

There was pandemonium, and those of us used to being at Wembley for FA Cup finals and England football internationals were convinced we had never heard a roar like the one that greeted Clay's knockdown. It was not so much like a clap of thunder as an animal growl coming from thousands of British throats. This was Last Night of the Proms xenophobia but with a savagery that would have rocked the bust of Proms founder Henry Wood off its plinth. Richard Burton's famous Welsh voice could be heard booming. 'Finish him Henry, finish him.' Liz Taylor was hiding her face.

Clay tried to show he was unhurt, but his senses were so scattered that he reeled back to his corner like a drunk on his way home from the pub. Dundee slapped his thighs as he sat him down on the stool, and as sponged water rained on Clay's head he instinctively tried to stand up as if to get back into the fight. What appeared to be illegal smelling salts were pressed under his nostrils and he pulled a grotesque face that made him look much older than his 21 years.

While all this was going on, the crafty and ring-wise Dundee was summoning over referee Tommy Little to show him that there was a split in Ali's right glove – not confessing until years later that he had made the split worse by digging in his thumb and pushing out horsehair.

Now we enter the world of myth and mystery. Many observers, including experienced boxing writers, claimed that Dundee's chicanery earned Clay an extra 20 to 30 seconds of recovery time. Even Henry, deluded by the reports, used to repeat the allegation in his after-dinner speeches.

Much as I would like to perpetuate the legend, I have to say I have been in the BBC archives department and watched the unedited version of the fight in real time. The interval between the fourth and fifth rounds actually lasted 66 seconds, which means that the Dundee gamesmanship gained just an extra six seconds.

Some reports even said that Clay had his glove changed, but there was not time for that before the bell rang to signal round five. Clay, now fully recovered, came out with the one intention of getting things finished before Henry could give him another taste of his hammer. A fusillade of lefts and rights landed on his damaged eye, and blood gushed as if being pumped out.

Liz Taylor, now brave enough to watch, was among the many ringside spectators screaming for referee Little to stop the fight. It was not a pretty sight.

After one minute 15 seconds of the fifth round and with Wicks up on the apron of the ring ready to throw in the towel, the referee waved his arms and called it off, saying to our bloody hero, 'Sorry, chum, the fight's over.'

CLAY AFTER-FIGHT QUOTE, 'Henry hit me so hard he shook up my ancestors in Africa. What this proves is that I can really take a punch, because that would have finished off most opponents. Henry is a proper English gent and has taken his defeat like the true sportsman he is. I apologise for calling him a cripple and a bum. He knew I was just trying to sell tickets, and it worked because this great stadium at Wembley is packed. Ninety-nine per cent of the crowd were rooting for Henry and wanted to see my big mouth shut. That made me all the more determined to win in style in the fifth, but the knockdown took the shine off my victory. Now for that big bum Liston and the world title.'

EYEWITNESS – HENRY COOPER (who often used the royal 'we'): "We didn't do bad for a bum and a cripple, did we! If only we had landed the left hook in the first minute of the round rather than the last we're convinced we would have knocked him out. We don't like blowing our own trumpet, but there were few who could match us for finishing off an opponent if we had him going … and Clay was out on his feet when he scrambled up. That showed his inexperience and also that he didn't know what day it was. He should have been looking to stay down for at least eight seconds. We know we'd have finished him off if the bell had not rung. He was also lucky to fall against the ropes. If I'd landed the punch when we were in the centre of the ring I don't think he would have got up in twenty seconds, let alone ten. Ali, as he became, often said that the sight of blood sickened him and that he wanted to look away when I was bleeding. He probably meant that in the cold light of day, but in the ring when it mattered he saw his advantage and came after me with an animal instinct for a finish. I was the prey and he was the hunter, and he wasn't going to let me go. And I don't blame him. The old fight game is not for faint-hearts. I would have done exactly the same thing in his boots. There were no bad feelings between us after it was all over. I knew he didn't mean half the things he said during the build-up to the fight. He was a master showman and did his job in getting bums on seats. To be honest, I really liked the bloke and always found him amusing company. He called himself The Greatest, and for many people he was but I think Joe Louis was probably the best heavyweight of them all. Clay or Ali or whatever you want to call him, was certainly the greatest entertainer."

Sonny Liston (USA)

**Venue: Miami Beach
25 February 1964
Clay 210lb, Liston 218lb
Clay WRET7
(Clay purse: $464,595)**

THE drums started beating for a Liston–Clay world championship showdown the minute the Cooper fight was over. That fourth-round knockdown strengthened the feeling in the Liston camp that Clay would be an easy defence, and they were persuaded to take him on in his adopted hometown of Miami.

Many considered Liston invincible after his two one-round wipeouts of former title-holder Floyd Patterson. It was a widespread feeling, and the knowledgeable Jim Wicks had said what many managers were thinking, 'I'd not let our 'Enery into the same room as Liston, let alone the same ring. He's an animal.'

The bookmakers agreed it was a certainty for Liston, and made him a 7/1 favourite. In a poll of leading sportswriters 43 of 46 picked Liston to win.

Clay used the publicity build-up to put huge psychological pressure on the moody champion. The colourful Bundini Brown – even more talkative than Cassius – had joined the Clay camp in the court jester role he used to play for Sugar Ray Robinson. He was the one who came up with the line, 'Float like a butterfly, sting like a bee...'

Brown was the motivator behind Clay, continually taunting Liston, because he knew it would not only sell tickets but also get under Sullen Sonny's skin. They bought a bus and had painted on the side, 'Sonny Liston Will Go In Eight'.

Clay and his entourage once drove the bus to the champion's Denver home in the middle of the night, and hooted the horn until a bad-tempered Liston came to the front door in his dressing gown and pyjamas. Clay was bashing dustbin lids together and shouting insults based on his new nickname for him, 'You big ugly bear...the traps are out for you and we're here to bait...'cos you're gonna fall in round eight.' It got to the point where seasoned convict Liston was threatening to call the police to report Clay for disturbing the peace.

For the first time the poison of politics came into the Clay world when, a month before the fight, he spoke at a Nation of Islam rally in New York City. Front page stories headlined that Clay was also spending a lot of time with controversial Nation of Islam minister Malcolm X, who was staying at a motel in Miami.

Bill McDonald, promoter of the title fight, feared that Clay's association with the Nation of Islam – which referred to white people as 'blue-eyed devils' – might hurt ticket sales. He threatened to cancel the contest unless Clay renounced the group. Cassius flatly refused.

McDonald decided to go ahead with the promotion only when Malcolm X was persuaded to leave town, and Clay agreed to delay an announcement about his Muslim affiliation until after the fight.

On the day of the fight, Clay seemed on the edge of hysteria during the official examination and weigh-in. His behaviour was so wildly out of control that the commission fined him $2,500. Clay's heart rate registered at 120 beats per minute and his blood pressure was 200/100. Dr Alexander Robbins, the chief physician of the Miami Boxing Commission, announced that he was 'emotionally unbalanced, scared to death, and liable to crack up before he enters the ring'.

He added that if Clay's blood pressure didn't return to normal, the fight should be cancelled. A second examination conducted an hour later revealed Clay's blood pressure and pulse were back to normal.

A calm, chilled Clay said that it had all been an act to unsettle the champion. 'Liston's not afraid of me,' he said, 'but he is afraid of a nut.'

His antics had captured the attention of the world, and huge audiences tuned in to see him start the fight at a helter-skelter pace, knocking Liston off balance with his fast and effective jab and rapid combinations. Liston looked ponderous by comparison, and was continually out of range with his feared left jab that had broken up a procession of opponents.

The champion was stalking, moving forward on flat feet. He fell short with two jabs, forced Clay back with a grazing right to the jaw and landed a solid right to the ribs. The crowd leaned forward as they sensed the imminent destruction of the young poet, but suddenly nothing rhymed for the champion as the Kid from Kentucky proved he was not exaggerating with his interminable refrains of 'float like a butterfly, sting like a bee'. He leaned back from Liston's jabs and hooks, backed on to the ropes, then spun out and away. He moved clockwise around Liston, taunting and mocking, his hands still low.

He had been floating, and then suddenly he stung, late in the first round, sticking his left in Liston's face and following with a quick barrage to the side of Sonny's head. They continued fighting for five seconds after the bell, unable to hear the ringing above the roar of the crowd.

There was a rare show of urgency from the champion at the start of the second as he lurched forward with desperate hooks that struck only air. For a moment, he pummelled Clay against the ropes, but again, he spun away as he shook his head in a mocking gesture.

Then the young challenger began to rumble as he had promised. His quick left jabs penetrated Liston's loose defence, and he followed with right hands. He leaned towards his rattled rival as he fired rights and lefts at Liston's expressionless face. The champion began to bleed from a crescent-shaped cut high on the left cheekbone.

Like a bull enraged by the picadors' lances, Liston charged forward. But the dodging, weaving, dancing Clay just skipped almost casually out of the way of his threatened big bombs that had destroyed Floyd Patterson in such dramatic fashion.

In the third round, Clay stopped running and started hitting with true power, causing a bruise under Liston's right eye to go with the cut under his left. The champion seemed to be aging by the minute.

Cassius coasted through round four and kept his distance while still peppering Liston with left jabs. As he returned to his corner at the bell, he started blinking as if having a fit, and complained in a literally blind panic that something was burning in his eyes and that he couldn't see.

Angelo Dundee rinsed Clay's eyes with a sponge and pushed him off his stool to begin the fifth round, telling him to stay away from Liston.

'I didn't know what the heck was going on,' Dundee revealed later. 'Cass said, "Cut the gloves off. I want to prove to the world there's been dirty work." And I said, "Whoa, whoa, back up baby. C'mon now, this is for the title, this is the Big Apple. What are you doing? Sit down!" So I get him down, I get the sponge and I pour the water into his eyes trying to cleanse whatever's there, but before I did that I put my pinkie in his eye and I put it into my eye. It burned like hell. There was something caustic in both eyes.'

Referee Barney Felix came towards Clay's corner as the challenger demanded that the fight be stopped. But Dundee waved him away and as the bell rang gave Clay the one-word instruction, 'Run!'

Many years later, Liston's cuts man Joe Pollino alleged that the champion ordered him to rub an astringent compound on his gloves before the fourth round, and he then rubbed his tainted gloves against Clay's eyes during a clinch.

Running around the ring like a scared rabbit, Clay survived the fifth round. His eyes had cleared by the sixth, when he resumed control of the fight against an opponent who was looking lost for what to do to catch his fleet-footed tormentor. The challenger was now standing his ground and hammering in a battery of effective combinations that rocked Liston's head back.

The weary champion slumped on his stool at the bell, telling his cornermen that he couldn't continue because of a shoulder injury. He failed to answer the bell for the seventh round and there was bedlam as Clay was declared the winner by technical knockout.

The new champion did a wild victory jig around the ring with his hands held high, and then leaned through the ropes and began yelling at the ringside media, 'I am The Greatest' and 'I shook up the world!'

Boxing would never be quite the same again.

Liston was taken to St Francis Hospital following the fight and emerged hours later with six stitches under his left eye and his left arm in a sling. Eight doctors certified that he had torn a shoulder muscle.

To this day controversy surrounds the way the fight finished, and it was recently revealed that the FBI investigated possible interference by the Mafia, but could find no concrete evidence. Common sense tells me that the Mob, with their well-publicised links with Liston, were hardly likely to give up the world title when it could be worth so much money in future defences.

I think it was a simple fact that bully boy Liston could not stomach being made to look a fool by a phenomenal fighter who was ready to live up to his self-styled title of The Greatest.

Three days after winning the title, Cassius Clay was no more. He announced to the world that he was a member of the Nation of Islam. and that in future he would answer to the name of Cassius X.

THE ALI FILES

On 6 March 1964, Elijah Muhammad announced that Cassius X would be renamed Muhammad Ali. 'Muhammad,' he explained, 'means "worthy of all praises", while Ali means "most high".'

CLAY AFTER-FIGHT QUOTE, 'Everybody's got to eat their words… all those people who said I did not belong in the same ring as that big ugly bear. They tried to cheat me by blinding me. But nothing was going to stop me taking that world title. Liston was too ugly to be the world's champ! The world's champ should be pretty like me! I've been telling you for years. Now you've gotta believe me. I am The Greatest.'

EYEWITNESS – SONNY LISTON, 'I still say the kid can't fight. I'll shut him up in the return when I'm fully fit.'

Sonny Liston (USA)

Venue: Lewiston, Maine
25 May 1965
Ali 206lb, Liston 215lb
Ali WKO1
(Ali purse: $361,819)

THE return match between Muhammad Ali – the Cassius Clay that was – and 'big, bad' Sonny Liston was the fight nobody wanted. State after state turned it down because of the stench that continued to surround their first fight, followed by Clay aligning with what many considered an anti-whites religious group. At this distance, you have to take into account the atmosphere of the time.

Their first fight had gone ahead just three months after the assassination of John F. Kennedy, and civil rights was still a raging issue. There were many restaurants in the Deep South that would not serve black people, and the United States was divided by fear and bigotry.

The return was originally scheduled for 16 November 1964 at The Boston Garden in Massachusetts, but three days before the contest Ali was rushed to hospital for an emergency hernia operation. The rematch was rescheduled for 25 May 1965, only for the Massachusetts authorities – along with the WBA – deciding to withdraw their sanction because of suspicions that the promoters were tied to organised crime.

Hawking the fight around the United States, they finally found an unlikely home in Lewiston, Maine's second largest city. The bout was staged at St Dominic's Hall in front of a crowd of 2,412, the smallest attendance ever for a world heavyweight championship fight.

To add to the edgy mood surrounding the showdown, three months before the fight Malcolm X had been assassinated following a violent falling out with the Nation of Islam. There were unsettling rumours that Malcolm X supporters were heading to Lewiston to gun down Ali, who had talked himself into being the Nation of Islam's most prominent member. There was a huge police presence at the arena and everybody was searched for weapons.

Following the unsatisfactory conclusion of their first fight, this return match had an even more controversial climax. Midway through the opening round, Liston threw a long, laboured left jab and Ali countered with a fast overarm right to the side of the jaw, catching Liston off balance and knocking him down. At first look, it seemed a stinging rather than concussive punch.

But it had scattered Liston's senses to the point that he was rolling on the canvas like a ship that had suddenly been holed. Ali stood over Liston, his right arm across his chest as if he was holding a sword and shouted, 'Get up and fight, sucker! We're on TV!'

Referee Jersey Joe Walcott, the world heavyweight champion until running into the fists of Rocky Marciano, looked as much at sea as Liston as he attempted to push Ali to a neutral corner.

Walcott was so preoccupied with trying to control the snarling, shouting, near-hysterical Ali that he failed to take up the count from the timekeeper. A bemused Liston struggled to his feet the little matter of 17 seconds after the punch landed and Walcott wiped his gloves and waved the fight back on.

At that moment, the confused Walcott heard renowned boxing scribe Nat Fleischer, publisher of *Ring Magazine*, who was sitting alongside the timekeeper, shouting, 'The fight's over, Joe.'

It had now become a pantomime as Walcott turned his back on the fighters to listen to Fleischer. Ali then started throwing punches at Liston, who raised his gloves to avoid the attack.

Fleischer, stopwatch in hand but not there in any official capacity, told Walcott that the timekeeper had counted to ten and that the fight was over. Jersey Joe responded by stepping between the fighters and raising Ali's hand in victory.

Ringside fans booed and started yelling, 'Fix! Fake!' Many did not see what became known as 'the phantom punch' land, and most of those who did see it connect didn't think it powerful enough to knock Liston out.

Expert ringside observers who had a clear view of the knockout punch were in no doubt about its power. 'It was a perfect right hand,' said Floyd Patterson. World light-heavyweight champion José Torres agreed. 'It was delivered with speed and strength and hit the spot,' he said. 'It was perfectly delivered against an opponent moving toward it, so that the effect was of a head-on collision.'

One who disagreed was future challenger George Chuvalo, who jumped into the ring during the pandemonium at the end shouting, 'Fix! No way was Liston knocked out. His eyes were darting from side to side while he was down. You don't do that when you're knocked out. Your eyes roll when you're ko'd. I've knocked out enough guys to know.'

An embarrassed Walcott said later, 'It didn't make any difference if I counted or not. I could have counted to 24. Liston was in a dream world, and the only thing that could have happened was that he'd be seriously hurt.'

'Chuvalo is wrong,' said Dr Carroll L. Witten, former Kentucky state boxing commissioner, who had studied the reactions of knocked-out fighters. 'The side-to-side movement of eyes is commonly associated with temporary unconsciousness and is one of the first things you look for. It is called nystagmus.'

In the wake of the Lewiston fight there was an outcry by press and politicians for the abolition of boxing. Bills to ban the sport were planned in several state legislatures, but Muhammad Ali was confident he was breathing life rather than death into the sport.

ALI AFTER-FIGHT QUOTE, 'Didn't I tell the world that I had a surprise and if I told you the surprise, you wouldn't come to the fight? It was a punch from beyond the grave, taught to me by [comedian/actor] Stepin Fetchit, who learned it from Jack Johnson. It's called "the anchor punch" and jarred Liston. Just more evidence that I truly am The Greatest. And now bring on the next challenger.'

EYEWITNESS – SONNY LISTON, 'I didn't think he could hit that hard. I was more confused than hurt. I got mixed up because the referee never gave me a count. I was listening for a count. That's the first thing you do, but I never heard a count because Clay wouldn't go to a neutral corner. Them's the rules.'

WHATEVER HAPPENED TO SONNY LISTON? Many theories were put forward that Charles 'Sonny' Liston took a dive in his second fight with Ali, including: (1) The Mafia forced him to throw the fight as part of a betting coup. (2) Liston bet against himself and took a dive because he owed money to the Mafia. (3) Liston was warned members of the Nation of Islam would kill him if he won the rematch. (4) Liston feared being shot by followers of Malcolm X as they tried to kill Ali in the ring. Old Sonny, the hoodlum who could never escape his past as a serial villain, took his secrets to the grave. He died in mysterious circumstances in December 1970, found dead by his wife in their Las Vegas home from an apparent heroin overdose. Allegations continue to this day that he was killed by the Mob. His ring record: 54 fights, 50 wins (39 inside the distance), four losses (three by knockout). Nobody ever knew his exact age because his birth in Arkansas – sometime probably in the late 1920s – was never registered. Sadly, he was the champion nobody loved.

Floyd Patterson (USA)

Venue: Las Vegas
22 November 1965
Ali 210lb, Patterson 197lb
Ali WRSF12
(Ali purse: $300,078)

MUHAMMAD ALI remembered a lesson he had been taught by master publicist 'Gorgeous' George Wagner, 'You earn more if you play the villain. Joe Public loves to hate.' He went out of his way to stoke up the loathing of white Americans against himself when he defended his world title against former champion Floyd Patterson in the gambling kingdom of Las Vegas.

He insulted and ridiculed Patterson at every opportunity, not only to get a psychological advantage over his opponent but also to sell tickets. Patterson told me on a visit to London the following year, 'Much of that was an act. Clay told me when the match was first made, "I'm going to say a lot of nasty things about you. Go along with it. Let's make some big bucks."'

But Ali took the verbal abuse to new extremes, calling Patterson 'The Rabbit' (because he's running scared), and painted him as 'an Uncle Tom, fighting for white America'. He was preparing to break with the syndicate of businessmen who had owned him, and his affairs would soon be handled by Nation of Islam leader Elijah Muhammad, whose son Jabir Herbert Muhammad was about to become his personal manager and spiritual adviser.

The fight was staged against the backdrop of a black freedom struggle rolling right across the USA. During the previous 12 months there were 1,000 arrests of civil rights activists, 30 buildings bombed and 36 churches burned by the Ku Klux Klan and their sympathisers. There were urban uprisings and riots in the northern ghettoes, and Ali fanned the flames of hatred.

Adding extra tension was the fact that the contest was taking place two years to the day that John F. Kennedy had been assassinated.

Patterson did not approach the fight quietly. 'I am on a crusade to reclaim the title from the Black Muslims,' he said in a rare show of out-of-the-ring aggression. 'As a Catholic I am fighting Clay as a patriotic duty. I am going to return the crown to America. The image of a Black Muslim as the world heavyweight champion disgraces the sport and the nation.'

Ali countered, 'Patterson says he's gonna bring the title back to America. If you don't believe the title is already in America, just see who collects my thousands of dollars in taxes. He sure as hell looks and sounds like that white guy, Uncle Sam. But he's more Uncle Tom.'

This was vitriolic stuff and went way beyond the usual ticket-selling scripts.

Torrential rain hit Vegas on the evening of the fight, and it was reported that $100 seats were being unloaded for $25. Ali's plan to be the villain worked because he was loudly booed into the ring while Patterson got a hero's welcome.

The challenger, desperate to regain the world title snatched away from him by his nemesis Sonny Liston, refused to call Ali anything but Cassius Clay, and this had him steaming. From the first bell he set out to humiliate the New Yorker, who throughout his career had represented boxing with dignity and good sportsmanship.

In the first round Clay showed Patterson total disdain in one of the most surreal starts to any world title fight. Boxing with his hands contemptuously down at his sides, he danced around the ring without throwing a single punch, offering his chin to Patterson and then just swaying out of range of his attempts at two-fisted attacks.

Ali was continually taunting his challenger, 'Come on American, come on white American…Come on Uncle Tom.'

A clearly exasperated Angelo Dundee told him at the end of the round, 'Champ, you are The Greatest, no doubt about it, but even you will have to hit your opponent to win a fight.'

Ali started to take it more seriously, and that was bad news for Patterson, who was on the receiving end of a systematic hammering round after round. He was beaten to the punch time and again, and his attempted counters were troubling only thin air. Every time he unveiled his famous kangaroo punch – leaping in to hook with both feet off the ground – Ali was just not there, leaning back and leering at flummoxed Floyd as the punch went whistling off target.

Patterson took a mandatory eight count in the sixth round when he briefly went down on one knee, with Ali's refusal to go to a neutral corner delaying the count. Throughout the fight Ali was booed and jeered for his arrogant behaviour against a clearly inferior but courageous opponent.

The seventh round – the one in which Ali had said he would end it – came and went with no change in the pattern of the fight, Ali dancin', jabbin' and gabbin', glidin' and slidin' and rocking the outgunned challenger with sudden swift combinations to the head.

It became evident that all was not well with Patterson, who was grimacing with pain halfway through the scheduled 15-rounder. We later learned that he had damaged a disc in his back during training, and the injury had returned.

The fight became embarrassing to watch as the crippled Patterson hobbled to his corner at the end of each round, while one of his seconds would grab him about the waist, lift him and squeeze him, desperately trying to alleviate the pain and get his back working properly.

In the 12th round, when it was painfully obvious Patterson had no hope of landing any sort of telling blow, Dundee – showing pity

– shouted from the corner, 'Ali, knock him out, for Christ's sake! Put him out of his misery.'

It looked as if Ali was deliberately punching him just enough to punish him but not to stop the fight, saying over and again, 'Come on Uncle Tom, you're fighting for white America…what's my name?'

Referee Harry Krause at long last signalled that the fight was over, saying later, 'I wanted to stop it in the 11th because it was hurting me to watch, but Patterson is such a good brave boy and has such a great heart, and I just couldn't do it. He so wanted to fight on, but he was going to get seriously hurt.'

ALI AFTER-FIGHT QUOTE, 'I told you all before the fight that it was a mis-match. He had no right to be in the same ring as me. Maybe he was a good champion once upon a time, but he is not in my class. He was disrespectful in refusing to acknowledge that I am now Muhammad Ali. I made him pay for that. I was not deliberately trying not to knock him out. The referee is in there to protect the boxers, and he should have moved in much earlier because I was punishing him in every round. Now he – and the whole world – knows what my proper name is.'

EYEWITNESS – FLOYD PATTERSON, 'I wanted to fight on. In my honest opinion, if I were watching the fight at home on TV, I'd have wanted it stopped, but I preferred to be counted out. Clay is an outstanding boxer, but does not have a hard punch. I kept it quiet that I had hurt my back in training because I thought I had got over the injury, but it came back at the worst possible time. I'm not going to make it an excuse, but you could see for yourself how it affected me. I've had a great career and I think I still have more to give. I have no plans to retire.'

George Chuvalo (Canada)

Venue: Toronto
29 March 1966
Ali 214lb, Chuvalo 216lb
Ali WPTS15
(Ali purse: $66,332)

ALI took on the entire United States establishment before this next defence, and was forced to leave the country to find venues where he could fight. He was scheduled to face the towering Ernie Terrell in Chicago on 29 March 1966, but shortly before the fight his draft classification was changed from 1-Y to 1-A, making him eligible for the US Army and a call-up to join the war in Vietnam.

Ali created a nuclear uproar by famously saying, 'I ain't got no quarrel with them Vietcong.'

He alienated much of white America when he added, 'I will not travel ten thousand miles to kill these dark Asiatic black people, who ain't done nothing to me. They ain't never called me nigger or threatened to lynch me or prevented me from drinking from a white water fountain. My fight is here in the United States to get equal rights for black folks.'

Ali was summoned before the Illinois State Athletic Commission to apologise for his 'unpatriotic remarks'. He refused to say he was sorry, and the Terrell fight was cancelled after the State Attorney General declared it 'illegal'.

Bob Arum, who had just started his first promotion company, Main Bout, was due to promote Ali–Terrell. He said later, 'I ran around the country without any luck looking for a state where we could have the fight. Finally, I took it to Montreal where we ran into politics and then it was on to Toronto. Terrell pulled out and we wound up with Ali–Chuvalo.' It was the first fight that Arum – future doyen of the boxing promoters – ever promoted.

On a cold, rain-drenched night in Toronto, Chuvalo battled his way forever into the hearts of his fellow Canadians and all fight fans that admire courage and character as he defied the so-called boxing experts and went the distance with the incomparable Ali in his prime.

Given only three weeks to prepare for the fight, the giant-hearted Chuvalo fought Muhammad Ali toe-to-toe for 15 savage rounds without taking a single backward step. He knocked the usual spring out of Ali's dancing and forced him to fight at close quarters, where his superior body punching caused the champion discomfort and a lot of pain that would later require hospital treatment for bruised kidneys.

Ali had nicknamed Chuvalo 'The Washerwoman' because of his two-fisted combinations that gave the impression of hands working a washboard. But no washerwoman ever hit as hard as Chuvalo, and the champion's attempts to taunt and tease the rock-like Canadian fell on deaf ears as Chuvalo dug deep for the performance of his life.

George – real name Juré Cuvalo, and born to Croatian parents – had chased Ali across America to try to needle him into giving him a title shot, even going so far as to invade a press conference dressed as a washerwoman. But his only gimmick when it came to the actual contest was to fight with all his heart and soul.

A favourite trick of Ali's was to push down with his left glove on his opponent's neck in clinches so that he could not function properly. Chuvalo turned this to his advantage, pounding away beneath Ali's left elbow with wicked right hand punches that dug deep into the midriff. Many of them landed in the back region, which brought protests from the Ali corner, where Bundini Brown was a noisy addition.

What Ali expected to be an easy workout – the world's press were unanimous in calling it a mismatch – developed into a war, and the scorecards (referee Jackie Silvers 73-65, judge Tony Canzano 74-63, judge Jackie Johnstone 74-62) did not tell the true story of how Chuvalo made Ali battle every inch of the way to retain his title.

ALI AFTER-FIGHT QUOTE, 'Chuvalo took everything I had and laughed at me. I don't think I hurt him once. He's got to be one of the hardest men on the planet, and he gave me the toughest fight of my life. Angelo told me to stop clowning, but no way was I clowning. I hit him with all I had but he just kept coming like a wild bull. I'm just glad we gave Canada a fight worth watching. I have been given a wonderful welcome here by very pleasant people, and was made to feel more at home than I am in my own country.'

EYEWITNESS – GEORGE CHUVALO, 'I gave it my best shot against an exceptional boxer. I made all those people who said I didn't belong in the same ring as Ali eat their words. He knows he's been in a fight and I bet he's going to feel my punches on his body for a long time. I think and hope that I did Canada proud. Now excuse me gentlemen, I've promised my wife that I'll dance the night away with her.'

Henry Cooper (GB)

Venue: Highbury Stadium, London
21 May 1966
Ali 201lb, Cooper 188lb
Ali WRSF6
(Ali purse: $448,186)

WITH controversy still raging in the United States about his refusal to join the US Army, Ali became a have-gloves-will-travel champion, and his next port of call was London and a return date with British hero Henry Cooper. It was an easy fight for promoter Harry Levene to sell because 'Enery's 'Ammer had famously floored Ali in his previous life as Cassius Clay, and Arsenal's Highbury stadium was heaving with 46,000 spectators. From the moment of the emotional singing of the national anthem there had been an air of optimism over Highbury that matched any from the Herbert Chapman days in the 1930s when Arsenal dominated league football. Everybody was trying to transmit their confidence and expectations to Henry, as Jim Wicks, trainer Danny Holland and brother George climbed out of the ring leaving our hero a lonely, proud figure up there in his corner awaiting the first bell.

Henry's wife, Albina, looking like a trapped prisoner in her first visit to a ringside, immediately looked away as Ali and Henry advanced towards each other. Alongside her, ring legends Rocky Marciano and Georges Carpentier leaned forward, eager to see if the modern boxers could match their deeds. Further along the row, the three greatest Welsh actors of their generation – Stanley Baker, Donald Houston and Richard Burton, all friends of Henry – chorused their support like members of a male voice choir.

For five rounds Henry forced the pace as Ali skipped and danced his way around the ballroom-size ring, the long laces on his snow-white boots twirling as he showed off the Ali shuffle. Once, twice, maybe three times Henry got home with the left hook that had dumped the then Cassius Clay on the canvas in their first meeting. But instead of going down, Ali had the presence of mind to grab and hold while his head cleared before getting back on his bike and into his rhythmic retreat behind long, stabbing punches that were quick enough to catch Henry in his tracks.

The bloody climax came in the sixth round with the dramatic suddenness of a landslide, just as we were thinking that Henry was on safe ground and that everything was going reasonably well.

As Henry tried to cut off Ali's retreat and drive him into a neutral corner he was suddenly met with an avalanche of short left- and right-hand punches to the face. It was a blur of combination punches that come from only the greatest fighters, and as Ali turned Henry on to the ropes ringsiders were sprayed with blood gushing from a wide-open gash along the so-often vulnerable left eyebrow. It was like an oil geyser exploding.

The oil was red.

A sideways glance showed that Albina was hiding her face behind her fight programme, wanting to be anywhere but at that ringside watching her husband suddenly looking like the victim of a car crash.

Wicks, Holland, brother George and matchmaker Mickey Duff were like a poorly tuned barber shop quartet as they screamed from the corner for Henry to make one last desperate attempt to land the 'ammer. But he was now blinded by a curtain of his own blood and missing wildly.

The roars from the crowd had gone from optimistic support to wild rage because many thought that a butt caused the damage. Even Henry made that instant allegation until he saw replays that showed the injury was definitely the result of a fusillade of deadly accurate punches.

There were soon cries of 'stop it ref' mixed in with the angry growls as Henry's blood ran like a red river down his chest and darkening his royal-blue shorts. Ali showed no mercy, and even though he later said he hated doing it he continued to pour punches into the widening wound. This was the blood sport of boxing at its most terrifying and repellent.

It was an astonishing turnaround. Barely a minute earlier Henry had been more than holding his own and was ahead on many scorecards. Now here he was drenched in his own blood.

Scottish referee George Smith, his shirt turning crimson, ushered Ali to a neutral corner and needed just a perfunctory inspection of the damage to wave the fight over. Henry punched the air in disgust and frustration and let fly with an expletive that edit-suite technicians carefully edited out.

The dream was over of becoming the first British-born fighter since New Zealand-based Bob Fitzsimmons back in 1897 to win the world heavyweight title, submerged beneath rivers of his blood. Yes, this was the unkindest cut of all.

ALI AFTER-FIGHT QUOTE, 'Henry hurt me just once. He caught me a good left hook in the third round, but I was far too fast for him tonight and he could not follow up. I opened the cut with a left-right combination. Henry is a man of honour and I'm sure that once he gets over the disappointment of his defeat he'll accept that I did not cause the damage with my head. With as pretty a face as I have, d'you think I'd go around butting opponents? Henry's a good fighter but his flesh is weak.'

EYEWITNESS – HENRY COOPER, 'In that sixth round we had been boxing at long range for about half a minute when he caught me as we both moved forward to launch punches, and as he moved away to continue his dance routine I felt blood oozing from a cut over my left eye. Immediately after the fight I told reporters there had been a clash of heads. I was not accusing the champion of doing it deliberately. He is not that type of dirty fighter. But my honest opinion was that the damage had been caused by his head. There was so much blood flowing that I could not believe it had been done by punches. Ali threw a right hand as I was coming in and something hard hit me.

'In the heat of the battle I thought he'd caught me with his nut. Afterwards, looking at the film, I could see I'd made a mistake and I later apologised to Ali for coming to the wrong conclusion. As in our first fight I was left thinking about what might have been. Most judges at the end either had me dead level or just in front on points, and I knew I had plenty in reserve. In eleven rounds of boxing Ali had never had me in serious trouble apart from the cuts. I'd had him down once and had won more rounds than I'd lost. I often wonder what I could have achieved but for the cut-eye curse.'

WHATEVER HAPPENED TO HENRY COOPER? Henry carried on fighting until he was 37, winning three Lonsdale belts outright and confirming his supremacy as the best heavyweight in Europe and the Commonwealth. He became a knight of St Gregory for his extensive charity work, and was also knighted by the Queen after a career in which he won 40 of 55 fights, 27 inside the distance. Seven of his 15 defeats came from eye injuries. He was considered a national treasure when he died following heart problems on May Day 2011, aged 76.

Brian London (GB)

Venue: Earls Court, London
6 August 1966
Ali 210lb, London 201lb
Ali WKO3
(Ali purse: $290,411)

ALI returned to London later in the summer of 1966 and polished off Brian London in three rounds on a Jack Solomons promotion at Earls Court that was a financial flop. The Blackpool boxer could never capture the public support like Our 'Enery. He lacked the famous Cooper charisma. Solomons had promoted the first Clay–Cooper fight and was spitting blood when he lost out on the return to his huge rival Harry Levene. In a moment of poor judgement he decided to bring Ali back to fight an opponent whose best was behind him.

There was a crowd of less than 10,000 in the cavernous Earls Court arena. Ali was on a guarantee of $252,000 plus a percentage of the TV revenue. London was paid a guaranteed $112,000. Famously careful with his money, London was not embarrassed when the day after the fight he was photographed buying a second-class train ticket home to the north-west.

Ali travelled first-class all the way, and he arrived in London for his training in time to be a guest at the World Cup Final.

While England were famously beating West Germany 4-2 after extra time the world champion was fast asleep at the back of the main Wembley stand! But he was wide awake for his fight against London, and it was the outclassed Brit who was knocked into slumberland. It is fair to describe it as a first-class boxer against an opponent giving a strictly second-class performance.

London talked a much better fight than he fought, and came out with a classic when asked before the fight how he would react if Ali started talking to him during the fight in his usual derogatory way. 'He can't insult me,' said London. 'I'm too ignorant.'

Not surprisingly, Ali in later life described his title defence against London as one of his easiest championship fights. It was annihilation, with the 'Blackpool Bomber' grounded almost from the first bell when he seemed to freeze with nerves.

He had managed to go 11 rounds of a title challenge against Patterson in Indianapolis in 1959 when he threw few attacking punches, and he came into the ring against Ali with the same defensive attitude. London was written off by the press, and the bookmakers rated him a 15/1 shot, which proved less than generous because Ali was hitting him 15 shots to one.

London tried stalking Ali but just ran into a hailstorm of leather as the champion danced in front of him with such supreme confidence that he was even content to often lead with his right.

In the second round London tried charging Ali into a corner, but found himself attacking the ropes as the champion skipped out of the way, laughing as if it was a playground game of tag.

Early in the third round Ali trapped 32-year-old London in his own corner, and delivered a devastating series of a dozen blows as if his opponent's head was a gymnasium speedball. As the blur of punches landed, London slumped down on his side and was counted out by referee Harry Gibbs after one minute and 40 seconds of the third round.

ALI AFTER-FIGHT QUOTE, 'I was impressed by the way London was talking coming into the fight, and I expected tougher opposition. But I punched too quick for him. My fists are the fastest in history. I have another fight lined up in five weeks' time here in Europe and so I wanted to get this over and done with quickly.'

EYEWITNESS – BRIAN LONDON, 'My plan was not to waste my strength and energy early on, and then come on strong in the later stages. But I could not believe the speed of his punches. They were like lightning. He calls himself The Greatest, and I think that's exactly what he is.'

WHATEVER HAPPENED TO BRIAN LONDON? Brian never made any secret that he was in boxing for one reason only, the money. His first question when offered a fight was always, 'How much?' He scored a shock points victory over world-ranked Zora Folley in 1967, but it was his last significant success. Brian, who had followed his father Jack London as British champion, failed to win one of his last six fights before retiring in May 1970 after a fifth-round stoppage by Joe Bugner. His ring record read: Fights 58, won 37 (26 inside the distance), lost 20, drew one. He opened a popular nightclub in Blackpool and as late as 2014 at the age of 79 was telling anybody who would listen that his proudest moment was sharing a ring with Muhammad Ali.

Karl Mildenberger (Germany)

Venue: Frankfurt
9 September 1966
Ali 204lb, Mildenberger 195lb
Ali WRSF12
(Ali purse: $211,576)

THERE were two firsts for Muhammad Ali in the sixth defence of his championship. In Karl Mildenberger he was meeting his first professional southpaw opponent, and this was the first world heavyweight title fight staged in Germany. Mildenberger was also making history by becoming the first southpaw to fight for the world heavyweight crown.

Legendary old championship rivals Joe Louis and Max Schmeling were reunited during the publicity build-up, and Ingemar Johansson flew in from Sweden to add to the big fight-night atmosphere.

Rather than the usual swapping of insults at the weigh-in, Mildenberger surprised Ali by asking for his autograph. Angelo Dundee said quietly to Bundini Brown, 'We're home free. This guy is in awe of Ali.'

But Dundee's expectations of an easy night proved over-optimistic and Ali had to dig deep to win a fight that exposed his unease against 'wrong-way-round' opponents. He had hired

Britain's Jack Bodell as a sparring partner but the German challenger was a much more skilful southpaw than the Swadlincote chicken farmer and made it difficult for Ali to carry out his promised 'float like a butterfly, sting like a bee' tactics. He spent much of the fight having to clinch and lean on the ropes as Mildenberger cut off his usual dancing route.

Ali had last fought a southpaw when winning the Olympic gold medal, and was inexperienced against a wrong-way-round opponent. Dundee kept reminding him that he should move away from Mildenberger's heavy right, and his usual rhythm was missing. It was like watching a thoroughbred racehorse that was slightly out of kilter.

Nearly two inches taller and ten pounds heavier than Mildenberger, Ali was installed as a 10/1 betting favourite and he comfortably won the first three rounds by scoring consistently with snaking left jabs and occasional snapping right leads to the head. But the European champion forced the pace, often connecting with his right jab and Ali seemed confused about how to find his punching range and accuracy.

Mildenberger increased his aggression in the fourth and fifth rounds and the Frankfurt crowd were just getting themselves worked into a frenzy when Ali scored a flash knockdown with a solid right to the head of the advancing German, who was troubled by a deep cut under his right eye.

Ali seemed in complete control as Mildenberger battled forward in the sixth with swollen eyes and blood flowing down his cheek, but the champion was forced to defend himself on the ropes in the seventh round against a two-fisted attack from the stubbornly brave challenger.

In round eight, the action swung dramatically Ali's way after he floored Mildenberger with a vicious left cross. Only the bell saved the German as the champion trapped him in a neutral corner with a volley of punches as British referee Teddy Waltham hovered ready to stop the fight.

Amazingly, Mildenberger recovered and was battling back when he was toppled by a huge right hand in the tenth round. The battered German was now fighting on instinct, and he was finally rescued after one minute and 28 seconds of the 12th as Ali sent him reeling with a volley of powerful punches.

ALI AFTER-FIGHT QUOTE, 'Mildenberger did himself and Germany proud. He gave me lots to worry about. His southpaw style was a problem, and he was amazing the way he kept coming back when I thought I had him beat. But I showed tonight I have courage and strength to go with my class.'

EYEWITNESS – KARL MILDENBERGER, 'I kept my promise to give Ali the hardest fight of his life. He is an extraordinary fighter but there were times in that ring tonight when he thought he was going to lose his world title. I know I really had him worried, but like all great champions he just found something extra every time I thought I'd got him. It was a privilege to share the same ring as him. He is a very special man and fighter.'

WHATEVER HAPPENED TO KARL MILDENBERGER? Karl kept fighting until losing in eight rounds to British hero Henry Cooper in a European championship fight in September 1968. His ring record: Fights 62, wins 53 (19 inside the distance), six defeats, three draws. He had distinctive snow-white hair as he approached old age and he remained a hugely popular hero with the German fight fraternity. Karl remembers his fight with Ali as the highlight of his career, and he kept in friendly contact with his old adversary.

Cleveland Williams (USA)

**Venue: Houston, Texas
14 November 1966
Ali 212lb, Williams 210lb
Ali WRSF3
(Ali purse: $405,000)**

F OR his first fight under the management of Herbert Muhammad, Ali returned home to the United States to face Cleveland 'Big Cat' Williams, who was something of a miracle man of the ring. Two years earlier he was shot in the stomach with a .357 magnum bullet from a policeman's revolver and he survived only after emergency surgery. But he had fought back to full fitness, and there were many in his adopted home state of Texas who thought he was going to prove too big a puncher for a champion still not forgiven for his refusal to join the US Army.

Ali had no doubts about the result, and before giving what is considered one of his most devastating performances he cockily announced, 'I beat the Bear and the Hare, and now I'll beat the Pussycat.' (Liston, Patterson, Williams, nicknamed Big Cat because of his huge physique.)

Fighting in the vast Houston Astrodome in front of a crowd of 35,460 – then the largest ever to witness a boxing match indoors –

Ali boxed with a confidence and arrogance that was breathtaking when you consider he was up against one of the most feared heavyweight punchers of his generation.

Circling quickly and snapping out what he called his 'sneaky, snaky' jab, Ali dominated from the first bell, making Williams appear slow as he plodded forward into a forest of punches. He was in mocking mood, and flaunted the Ali shuffle that had become a showboating part of his repertoire.

There was a hint of the demolition to come in the second round when the hounded Williams took three counts, seeking shelter on the canvas rather than face the blur of leather coming his way. He was flat on his back and looking down and out when the bell saved him.

The challenger was spitting blood at the start of the third round as Ali hit him with a barrage of punches that had even Big Cat's supporters in the crowd shouting for the fight to be stopped. This was Ali at his majestic best and most merciless.

Williams, who had hardly landed a punch of note, unwisely tried one counter attack, and all it brought him was more punishment. A crashing left hook floored him for a fourth time, and as he pluckily clambered up blood was streaming from his mouth. He staggered forward into another burst of two-fisted fire, and one punch twisted him around so that his back was towards his relentless assailant. As Ali sent him floundering around the ring, referee Harry Kessler stepped in to end what had become a sickening slaughter.

ALI AFTER-FIGHT QUOTE, 'I deliberately came in heavy at 212 pounds so that I would be able to hit hard. And I did. But carrying that extra weight made me tired and I was happy when the referee stepped in. I was nearly exhausted from hitting him. Is there anybody anywhere in the world now who does not believe I am The Greatest? Ernie Terrell's next. He was ringside tonight and saw just how great I am. He's in for a real beating, just like the one I gave Williams.'

THE ALI FILES

EYEWITNESS - CLEVELAND WILLIAMS, 'I don't remember much after he hit me with a right in the first round. It scrambled me and I couldn't do all the things I had planned. He caught me before I'd really got started. I have only myself to blame. I dropped my left hand and left my chin unguarded. That was a silly thing to do and I paid the price. That's it for me. I'm hanging up my gloves. Pity I didn't go out a winner. I was convinced I could knock Ali out, but he moves so fast that all I did was give his shadow a good hiding.'

WHATEVER HAPPENED TO CLEVELAND WILLIAMS? The Big Cat kept his promise to retire, but financial debts forced a comeback. Although able to defeat journeymen fighters, he suffered several knockout losses when climbing into the ring with contenders who used him as a stepping stone to title challenges. He pulled out of a fight with Dick Richardson in London because he said he had heard a message from God telling him not to box.

Cleveland retired for good in 1972. He finished his career with the ring record: Fights 92, 78 wins (58 inside the distance), 13 losses and one draw. The police shooting incident, when he was falsely arrested on a drunk-driving charge, left him with damaged kidneys and on 3 September 1999 he was leaving hospital after a dialysis session when he was knocked over and killed by a hit and run driver. Aged 66, he had not been the luckiest of men.

Ernie Terrell (USA)

Venue: Houston, Texas
6 February 1967
Ali 212lb, Terrell 212lb
Ali WPTS15
(Ali purse: $585,000)

WITH the accusations of being a draft dodger reaching a crescendo across the United States, Ali was proving one of the most controversial heavyweight champions in history as he prepared for his unification title fight with the towering Ernie Terrell.

It developed into one of the cruellest championship contests ever witnessed as Ali, at his most sadistic and brutal, kept his vow to humiliate Terrell for refusing to acknowledge his new identity as Muhammad Ali.

In a deliberate attempt to needle and unsettle Ali, Terrell kept calling him Cassius Clay during the preliminaries before the fight. This was not a ticket-selling gimmick. These were two giants engaging in a war of words, and with an undercurrent of real hatred.

Ali's eyes blazed with anger as he said to Terrell, 'My name is Muhammad Ali and you will announce it right there in the centre of that ring after the fight, if you don't do it now. You are acting

101

just like an old Uncle Tom, another Floyd Patterson. I'm gonna punish you so bad you will be begging for mercy and calling out my real name for the whole world to hear.'

Terrell, a professional rock singer and guitarist when not boxing, was not in tune with Ali and replied, 'I've known you since back in the amateurs and to me you are still Cassius Clay.'

When it came to fight night in front of a 37,321 audience at the Houston Astrodome and millions more on closed-circuit and worldwide television Ali provided action to go with his words, while Terrell was given the hiding of his life. He was suddenly in the mood to sing the blues.

In the opening rounds Ali moved cautiously, staying carefully beyond the range of his 6ft 6in opponent's long left jabs. In the second round he opened a small cut under Terrell's left eye and his right eye started to puff up. These injuries were to become the cause of huge controversy.

'Clay rubbed my eye against the top rope in the second round,' Terrell complained later. 'He rubbed one eye on the rope and put his thumb in the other eye, and for the rest of the fight I was seeing two or three of him. His speed didn't bother me and he didn't hurt me with his punching, but I couldn't see him. I was fighting half blind.'

There was no indication of his handicap as in the fourth round he hit Ali with a sharp right cross. Ali slid away along the ropes and countered with a left, but Terrell hit him again with the right before the Kentuckian could escape. Muhammad weathered a storm of lefts and rights in this exchange by clever shifts of his head and swift, slick footwork. This was to be the last decent attack from Terrell.

Ali took complete command from the fifth round, jabbing and jarring Terrell with solid left leads and then mixing in a cluster of two-fisted hooks and uppercuts that continually rocked the fighting musician back on to his heels.

Early in the seventh, now fighting close to Terrell and no longer concerned about the difference in reach, Ali unleashed a bombardment of punches against the side of his opponent's head, then almost lifted him off his feet with a short, powerful right uppercut. The following punch opened a deep, bloody gash over Terrell's right eye and he staggered like a drunken man across the ring, where he was kept upright by the ropes. Ali then hit him in the face again, this time with a violent left hook.

Instead of going in for a knockout, Ali stepped back and was heard shouting, 'What's ma name?'

This became the pattern of the rest of the fight, Ali punching Terrell to the edge of unconsciousness and then pulling back and asking, 'What's ma name? What's ma NEW name?'

Bleeding heavily and in a constant daze, Terrell concentrated on survival and trying to avoid as many of the battery of punches as possible.

Ali was taunting and torturing Terrell, exactly as he had threatened. 'You're an Uncle Tom,' he said while landing a tattoo of lefts and rights. 'Tell me ma name.'

It was obvious he was deliberately pulling back every time he was on the point of knocking out his bruised and battered opponent. Many in the crowd, wincing at the flow of blood and unanswered punches, were yelling for it to be stopped. But Terrell was no quitter and he shuffled forward courageously, peering through what were now the slits of his eyes while Ali baited him, moving just beyond his reach and hitting him at will.

At the beginning of the tenth round Ali stood in front of Terrell and tapped himself on the jaw, indicating that this was where the blow would land to knock out the WBA champion in the round that he had predicted. But he appeared to change his mind and just seemed content to punish Terrell even more with a combination of punches and insults.

Between the 13th and 14th rounds referee Harry Kessler summoned a doctor to examine Terrell's right eye, but surprisingly the barbarically one-sided bout was allowed to continue to what was an inevitable points victory for Ali. It was scored: Referee Harry Kessler 148-137, judge Jimmy Webb 148-133, judge Ernie

Taylor 148-137. It was a walkover victory, but left a bad taste in the mouth – and many bruises on the outclassed Terrell.

ALI AFTER-FIGHT QUOTE, 'I did what I said I'd do. I gave him a lesson. He never hurt me. My only concern was not exhausting myself from hitting him. Never reached me with that left jab of his. I don't know what I hit him with, 'cos there were too many punches to count. I got to say he's a brave man. I jes' couldn't put him down, so I had to back off now and then and get my breath. I think he and everybody now knows my name.'

EYEWITNESS – ERNIE TERRELL, 'I was seeing three of him from the second round after he had thumbed one eye and rubbed the other one on the rope. Clay is a very good fighter, but I think all those who watched him in this fight now knows there is a side of him that is extremely nasty. Is that what we want from our world champion? Is that the way to win a fight? I have no respect for the man, and would willingly fight him again. I am sure I could beat him if I was not blinded. And I will continue to call him Cassius Clay.'

WHATEVER HAPPENED TO ERNIE TERRELL? Ernie retired in 1973 after 55 professional fights, with 46 wins (21 inside the distance), and nine losses. He went full-time into music, starting his own record production company in his adopted home city of Chicago. He sang and played guitar with his group Ernie Terrell and the Heavyweights, and duetted with his sister Jean Terrell, who replaced Diana Ross as lead singer with The Supremes. In 1987 he ran for alderman in Chicago's 34th Ward but was beaten in a run-off. When he retired, he mellowed into an affable and likeable bear of a man, who talked warmly and with respect for his old foe, 'Cassius Clay aka Muhammad Ali'. He was inducted into the World Boxing Hall of Fame in 2004. Like so many before him, Ernie did not know when to get off the mountain and was lost in the fog of dementia when he passed on in December 2014, aged 75.

Zora Folley (USA)

Venue: Madison Square Garden, NY
22 March 1967
Ali 211lb, Folley 202lb
Ali WKO7
(Ali purse: $275,000)

STICKING to his principles, Muhammad Ali would not budge on his refusal to be drafted into the US Army. He was ready to pay the price of a prison sentence and the surrender of his world championship. This would be his last fight for three-and-a-half years.

In the opposite corner stood Zora Folley, the number one contender who had been knocking at the championship door for several years and, at 34, was past his peak. Born in Dallas, Texas, he was brought up in Chandler, Arizona, where he was a noted baseball player.

Folley joined the US Army in 1948, and switched to boxing as his main sport after winning the All-Army and All-Service titles. Contrasting what was now happening to Ali, he fought in the Korean War, earning five battle stars.

He launched a successful professional career and was lined up for a world title challenge against Floyd Patterson until Britain's Henry Cooper threw a hammer in the works with a points victory in London in 1958. Folley beat such contenders as Eddie Machen, George Chuvalo, Oscar Bonavena, and Doug Jones. He also drew with Karl Mildenberger and avenged the defeat by Cooper with a second-round knockout. But his world title ambitions stalled with stoppages by Sonny Liston, Alejandro Lavorante, and – in a rematch – Doug Jones. Following a points loss to Ernie Terrell in the summer of 1963 he went 12 successive fights without defeat to earn his shot at Ali.

He paid Ali the respect of referring to him by his new name, and the champion jokingly complained that he could not work up any hatred against father-of-nine Folley. But such was the interest in his battle with the US government that the fight drew a crowd of 13,780 and set new Madison Square Garden gate receipts of $244,471.

A supremely confident Ali appeared to play with Folley in the first two rounds and it wasn't until the third that he started to show serious intent. His suddenly powerful rather than flicked left jabs kept snapping Folley's head back. In the fourth, there was a dramatic change in Ali's attitude. He stopped dancing and planted his feet, getting full leverage into his punches. A left hook spun Folley around and a following right hand landed just behind his ear. Zora flopped flat on his stomach, and then – his nose streaming blood – took a nine count on his knees after spinning round to look to his corner.

Folley bravely survived until the seventh when two vicious rights to the head in quick succession sent him face first to the canvas for the full ten-second count.

All the talk was now about Ali's future and his ongoing battle against joining the US Army. His management cancelled a planned 27 May fight with Oscar Bonavena in Tokyo after his appeal on the grounds that he was a Muslim minister and conscientious objector had been refused. He had managed to make himself at one and the same time one of the most hated and admired men in an American nation split on the topic of the war in Vietnam. Now he had surrendered the one platform from which he could preach his message to the world, the boxing ring.

ALI AFTER-FIGHT QUOTE, 'This may have been the last chance to see Muhammad Ali in living colour. Perhaps in one to three years I will fight again, only Allah knows. My life, my death, all my sacrifices are for Allah. I am the tool of Allah and because of my sacrifice it will come out that hundreds of Muslims are in jail rather than fight in the Army. After I go, boxing will be a graveyard.'

EYEWITNESS – ZORA FOLLEY, 'The first time I went down, I wasn't hurt, but I didn't know what had happened. Suddenly I became aware of Ali standing over me, and I figured I was down. So I wheeled around to look at my corner, to find out the count. I kept thinking, was that a right hand he hit me with? So what did he do but hit me with the same punch again in the seventh round and knock me out. I can't believe it, but that's what he did. He's smart. The trickiest fighter I've seen. He could write the book on boxing, and anyone that fights him would be wise to read it first.'

WHATEVER HAPPENED TO ZORA FOLLEY? Zora fought for three more years before hanging up his gloves after being knocked out in the first round by Mac Foster in 1970. He was keen on community work and served as a member of the Chandler City Council in Arizona. Visiting a friend in Tucson on 8 July 1972, he suffered severe head injuries in a motel swimming pool incident and died at a Tucson hospital. The death was officially ruled to be accidental, but conspiracy theories regarding his death persist. The city of Chandler dedicated Zora Folley Memorial Park in his honour. Zora's ring record: Fights 96, won 79 (44 inside the distance), lost 11, drew six.

Jerry Quarry (USA)

**Venue: Atlanta, Georgia
26 October 1970
Ali 213lb, Quarry 197lb
Ali WRSF3
(Ali purse: $580,000)**

LEGAL eagles in the courtroom did all of Ali's fighting for the following three years. It took his 43-month banishment from the ring – as the body bags continued to be flown home from Vietnam – for the public sentiment to change. There was a huge mood swing against the war, and the man branded a traitor was turning into a hero with many young Americans.

When Ali had his boxing licence withdrawn in 1967 for refusing to be drafted into the Vietnam War, the World Boxing Association organised an elimination tournament to decide a new champion.

Jerry Quarry reached the final by outpointing Floyd Patterson and then stopping the highly regarded Thad Spencer in the 12th round. But he was then outpointed by Ali's Louisville friend Jimmy Ellis in a dull, uneventful 15-round battle for the vacant title.

Manager Herbert Muhammad tried to set up a showdown with Ellis during Ali's exile, which would have been held in an empty arena to beat the nationwide ban but shown on closed-circuit television. The plan collapsed when Ellis was flattened by Joe Frazier in a unification fight.

To keep himself occupied during his exile, Ali hit the campus trail as a hugely in-demand college lecturer, and he appeared on Broadway in the musical *Buck White*. But he was aching to get back into the ring, convinced he could show the world he was still The Greatest.

How ironic that it was the state of Georgia that broke ranks and agreed to stage Ali's return to the ring. Its governor, Lester Maddox, had been a fierce opponent of the civil rights movement that had Ali as one of its heroes. His comeback fight against Quarry was screened on closed-circuit TV in 206 locations in the United States and Canada, and was also beamed live to Asia, Australia, Europe and South America.

There was a sell-out crowd of 5,100 at Atlanta's old Municipal Auditorium, with a celebrity-packed audience including VIP black supporters Jesse Jackson, Sidney Poitier, Arthur Ashe, Bill Cosby, Diana Ross and the Supremes, the Temptations and the widow of Martin Luther King, who had been assassinated during Ali's enforced lay-off. The *New Yorker* essayist George Plimpton was an eyewitness who remembered 'an invasion of Harlem peacocks in their enormous purple Cadillacs...I'd never seen crowds as fancy, especially the men – felt hatbands and feathered capes, and the stilted shoes, the heels like polished ebony, and many smoking stuff in odd meerschaum pipes.'

It was almost as if Ali had never been away as he danced around the ring for two rounds, bewildering the power-punching Quarry with the blinding speed of his footwork and his rat-a-tat attacks that had helped him defeat his previous 29 opponents. It was the first time Ali had fought a younger opponent, and he was making 25-year-old Quarry look old before his time.

Quarry seemed perplexed by the swiftness of Ali's movement, and he was unable to launch an effective attack. He was off target with attempted counters, hurling wild hooks, most of which missed or were brushed off. He landed just one telling punch – a solid right hand to the body in the second round that made Ali briefly look to clinch.

The third round was following the same route with Ali in control when he followed a series of sharp jabs with a corkscrewing right over a tentative left lead. The second it landed above Quarry's left eye there was a tell-tale sign of blood, and the Californian started dabbing at the wound as Ali made it worse with his accurate two-fisted attacks.

At the end of the round referee Tony Perez followed Quarry to his corner and, after a discussion with his chief second Teddy Bentham, waved the fight over, with Ali consoling a desperately disappointed opponent. It was a deep, jagged cut that required 15 stitches.

ALI AFTER-FIGHT QUOTE, 'I didn't want it to end that way, but I knew it was a bad cut and there was nothing they could do to stop the blood running into the eye. Jerry was a respectful opponent and was giving a good account of himself. I needed the action and will be proving that I've come back better than ever. I'm on Frazier's trail.'

EYEWITNESS – JERRY QUARRY, 'I don't want to hear anybody saying the cut was caused by a head butt. It was a punch that did it, a right hand. The minute it landed I knew I was in trouble. I had not really got into the fight and had so much more to give. But I welcome Ali back. He's good for boxing. Obviously I'd like to have another crack at him.'

Oscar Bonavena (Argentina)

Venue: Madison Square Garden, NY
7 December 1970
Ali 212lb, Bonavena 204lb
Ali WRSF15
(Ali purse: $925,000)

THE traps were being set for a showdown with Smokin' Joe Frazier, but Angelo Dundee wanted Ali to get more rounds under his belt following the long, rust-forming lay-off. His nine minutes of one-sided action against Jerry Quarry hardly got his motor warmed up, and when Leotis Martin vacated the NABF heavyweight title the Ali camp negotiated to fight Argentine iron man Oscar Bonavena for the vacant crown.

Bonavena, nicknamed Ringo, was something of a screwball; an extraordinary character who was a hard-drinking playboy and like a ticking time-bomb both inside and outside the ring. He was as strong as an ox, and did not know the meaning of fear or retreat. His style of fighting was crude but effective, and he had never taken a count in 52 fights when he agreed to cross swords with Ali.

The man who had put Frazier down twice in a war that he lost on points matched Ali with his tongue as they set about selling out Madison Square Garden.

Making a noise like a clucking chicken, he said to Ali's face, 'Why you no go in Army? You big chicken. Chicken! You big chicken! Chicken!'

They had 150 nationwide closed-circuit theatres to fill, and Ali stoked up the fires of what was really fake hatred. 'Please,' he said at every opportunity, 'tell everyone to get to the theaters. I have never had a man that I wanted to whup so bad!'

Ali predicted he would stop Bonavena in nine rounds. 'He'll be mine in nine,' he kept repeating right up until the first bell.

But it took 15 rounds before he could finally tame the wild bull of Buenos Aires. It really was like a matador against the bull from the first bell, with Ali dancing and flicking out left leads mixed with sudden bursts of two-fisted combinations as the wide-shouldered Bonavena lumbered forward, seemingly unaffected by the constant barrage of punches coming his way.

Apart from one left hook that had Ali briefly wobbling, the Argentine rarely troubled the Kentuckian, who was being less cocky than usual as he concentrated on trying to stop his opponent's aggressive march. In the second half of the fight, Bonavena started to have more success with his roughhouse tactics and it was clear that Ali was tiring and lacking his old strength and stamina.

Just when everybody thought he was settling for a points victory, Ali unleashed a whiplash left hook a minute into the final round that sent Bonavena tumbling to the canvas for the first count of his career. Ali broke the rules by not going to a neutral corner and was within punching range as a shaken Oscar got to his feet to be met by a left and a right that dumped him back on the seat of his trunks.

Again Ali was loitering with intent instead of going to a neutral corner, and crashed in two more punches that sent Bonavena down for a third time that signalled an automatic stoppage.

Going into that 15th round, referee Mark Cohen's scorecard had Ali ahead 12-2, judge Joe Eppey scored it 10-3-1, and judge Jack Bloom had him leading 8-5-1.

ALI AFTER-FIGHT QUOTE, 'I needed that 15 rounds to prove I still had stamina. Joe Frazier couldn't put Bonavena down. I did it three times, so now you know I have the punch to take out Joe. Oscar has a strong chin and a big heart and I like the man. But I did what I had to do, and now I'm ready to take my world title back. I am breathing life back into boxing. It was dead while I was away.'

EYEWITNESS – OSCAR BONAVENA, 'I have apologised to Ali for calling him a chicken. That was all to help the publicity. He is a very brave man and a fine boxer. Nobody has ever knocked me down before. I admire him, and he really is The Greatest. He is a sure thing to beat Frazier.'

WHATEVER HAPPENED TO OSCAR BONAVENA? This was the only time Oscar was stopped in 68 fights, 58 of which he won. It was his crazy behaviour outside the ring that ultimately led to his premature death in May 1976, aged 33. He got involved in a scandal at the notorious Mustang Ranch Brothel in Nevada. According to reports, Bonavena had an affair with the brothel owner's wife, 26 years his senior. One of the owner's bodyguards shot Bonavena through the heart during an altercation. Still idolised in Argentina, his body lay in state at the Luna Park Sports Arena in Buenos Aires where 150,000 mourners filed by to pay their respects. A statue was built in memory of a flawed hero.

Joe Frazier (USA)

Venue: Madison Square Garden, NY
8 March 1971
Ali 215lb, Frazier 205lb
Ali LPTS15
(Ali purse: $2.5m)

THIS was the first of the truly iconic Ali contests, living up to its billing as the 'fight of the century'. It takes two to tangle, and coming from the opposite corner was Smokin' Joe Frazier, a brawler, a mauler, a born warrior who was to become Ali's nemesis over a three-fight series that captured the imagination and interest of the world and pushed both men to new heights of endeavour and new pits of pain. Somebody's unbeaten record was going to have to go.

It was not just a fight night. It was an occasion, a sports event that could rate with a World Cup Final, a World Series baseball showdown, a Beatles concert, a Sinatra show. Oh, hold on, Sinatra was there, but because he could not get a ticket he talked himself into a role as ringside photographer for *Life*.

The capacity-crammed Madison Square Garden had a coronation-like atmosphere, with hundreds of policemen controlling a crowd of fashionably dressed fans, and countless celebrities, from Norman Mailer and Woody Allen to Burt

Lancaster working as a colour commentator for the closed-circuit broadcast alongside Ageless Archie Moore. Master artist LeRoy Neiman painted the scenes for what was then considered the fight of the century.

Ali and Frazier agreed to split the then record $5million purse equally, and then overworked their tongues to get the arena seats and worldwide theatres filled. There was a riot in Chicago where a power cut shut off the picture in the third round, and the fuming audience smashed up the theatre.

The fight captured the mood of the times. Ali's refusal to fight in Vietnam had turned him into a symbol of the anti-establishment movement. Meanwhile, Frazier was presented as representing the conservative, pro-war movement. Or, as Ali taunted him, 'You're an Uncle Tom…fighting for the white man.'

Writing as a former boxing PR, I can assure you that much of their pre-fight anger and aggravation was carefully choreographed by the publicists, but Ali being Ali he could not resist putting in deeply insulting comments designed to get under the skin and give him a psychological advantage.

As they prepared to listen to the final instructions from referee Arthur Mercante, Ali leaned into Frazier and said, 'You know, you're in here with God tonight.'

'Well, if you're God,' Frazier responded, 'you're in the wrong place tonight.'

It was the first of many great counters from the champion.

The fight exceeded even the promotional hype. Ali, up on his toes and moving with a rhythm to which Sinatra could have sung a song for swinging glovers, monopolised the first three rounds, irritating and outwitting the shorter, stockier Frazier, decorating his face with rapier-like jabs that raised welts on the champion's cheeks. Then, like a clap of thunder, Frazier announced his serious participation in the closing seconds of round three in the shape of a tremendous left hook to Ali's jaw that snapped the challenger's head back. Frazier then switched a venomous attack to Ali's body and he was forced to take cover behind raised arms for the first time.

Frazier began to dominate from the fourth round, finding the range with his famed and feared hooks and pinning Ali against the ropes while delivering heavy body blows. As the fight reached the sixth round at a furious pace we onlookers started to realise that this fight had come too early on Ali's comeback trail. He was visibly tired and started fighting in flurries, while looking for every chance to rest against the ropes while catching his breath.

The fight was close and difficult to call until late in round 11 when the perpetual-motion Frazier hooked Ali to the head and followed with a vicious left to the body that sent the challenger rolling back to a neutral corner, like a swimmer suddenly caught in a tidal wave. He hung on for dear life as Frazier stepped up his non-stop attack. This was the moment when only the most optimistic Ali fans thought he could still scale the mountain.

At the bell, Angelo Dundee met him with a sponge of water in his face before he could reach his corner. There, with his 'witch doctor', Bundini, desperately trying to motivate him, and Angelo suggesting hit and run tactics, Ali attempted to regain his scattered senses.

As he came out for the 12th, there was an audible gasp from ringsiders as they saw that the right side of Ali's face was grotesquely swollen and it seemed his jaw was broken. He used every defensive trick in the book to stop Frazier adding to his pain, and in the 13th round took refuge in a neutral corner, concentrating on avoiding punches while down below him an almost weeping and wailing Bundini Brown was yelling as if at a religious convention. 'You've got God in your corner, Champ!' he kept shouting. 'Shorty's with you.'

Ali briefly came back to life in the 14th, but it was clear he was going to have to drag up a knockout blow if he was to rip the title from the ferocious Frazier. But the nearest to a finishing punch came from the champion in the frantic 15th and final round. He exploded a left hook to the right side of Ali's chin, sending him crashing to the canvas with his head ricocheting off the floor, his feet flailing in the air.

Miraculously he got up and stumbled through the final minute in what had now become a damage limitation exercise. He knew in his heart that his chances of taking the title from Frazier had gone. The 1964 Olympic heavyweight champion had been too mean and hungry for the 1960 Olympic light-heavyweight gold medallist.

We did not have to wait long for confirmation that, by a unanimous decision, the winner and STILL world heavyweight champion was Joe Frazier. Several good judges at the ringside scored it a draw, but the official result was: Judge Artie Aidala 9-6, judge Bill Recht 11-4, referee Arthur Mercante 8-6.

That was it. Until the next time. And the time after that. They did it again. And again, while we mere mortals looked on open-mouthed in wonderment.

ALI AFTER-FIGHT QUOTE, 'Joe's broken my jaw but not my heart. I now know I could have done with a couple of more fights to get the rust out. I'm not going to cry. I made a lot of people unhappy when I beat them, so it's my time now. A lot of great fighters get whipped. No one can hit as hard as Frazier. I'm satisfied with the fight even though I lost. I know I lost to a great champion, but maybe another time when both of us had been fighting regularly, the result would have been different. I don't know, but maybe.'

EYEWITNESS – JOE FRAZIER, 'That man can sure take some punches. I went to the country, back home, for some of the shots I hit him with. When I heard the final bell, I looked at Ali and said, "Yeah, I kicked ya' ass." He ain't The Greatest. He's been kiddin' himself and the world all these years. It became my mission to show him the error of his foolish pride. Beat it into him. And that's exactly what I did. I beat him up real good. I shut his big mouth.'

Jimmy Ellis (USA)

**Venue: Houston, Texas
26 July 1971
Ali 220lb, Ellis 189lb
Ali WRSF12
(Ali purse: $450,000)**

THE comeback fight for Ali after his painful defeat by Frazier was one he would rather have ducked. It meant he would be hitting and hurting one of his closest friends. He and Jimmy Ellis had grown up together in Louisville, went to the same high school, and fought each other twice as amateurs. Ali won the first bout, and Ellis the return.

Ali often hired Ellis as a sparring partner to help boost his earnings, and they were both trained by Angelo Dundee. After torturing himself, Angelo decided his duty was to be in the corner of the underdog Ellis, whom he also managed. Ali gave Dundee his blessing and got the renowned veteran trainer Harry Wiley, who had worked with Henry Armstrong and Sugar Ray Robinson, to be his stand-in chief second.

They battled for the NABF title that had been vacated by George Foreman, and there was so much interest in how Ali would be affected by his pounding from Frazier that the Houston Astrodome was packed with 31,947 spectators.

Ellis had the skill to compete at the top level, but not the raw power to survive against the really big punchers. Joe Frazier and Earnie Shavers both took him out with their savage blows.

He sparred hundreds of rounds with Ali in the gymnasium, and knew his style and tricks better than anybody. While few gave him a chance of scoring an upset victory, he started with a flourish and for the first three rounds controlled the exchanges with Ali-style movement and quick fists.

But the fight dramatically swung Ali's way from the moment late in the fourth round when a chopping right hand hit Ellis flush on the side of the jaw and turned his legs to rubber. He staggered around the ring under fire until the bell came to his rescue.

Ali, at 220lb, was at his heaviest and looked even bigger because Bundini Brown had forgotten to pack his trunks, and the pair borrowed at the last minute were two sizes too large. But while carrying extra weight, Ali was more on his toes than when he fought Frazier and started to take complete control after the near stoppage at the end of the fourth round.

He stepped up the pace from the halfway mark and was continually beating Ellis to the punch with left jabs that were snappy and accurate. In round 12 he stopped what had almost become exhibition boxing and switched to power hitting, threatening to lift Ellis out of his boots with a thumping right uppercut that parted him from his senses.

Ali, clearly hoping that referee Jay Edson would intervene, then threw a combination that left Ellis helpless on the ropes, and stood back as he virtually invited Edson to step in and stop the fight at two minutes and ten seconds of the 12th round.

ALI AFTER-FIGHT QUOTE, 'Next to me, Jimmy is the best heavyweight boxer in the world. I showed I'm getting into the shape to take Frazier next time we meet. I could've knocked Jimmy out in the 12th round but there ain't no reason for me to kill nobody in the ring. I was just waiting for the referee to stop it, not because Jimmy's my friend but because he's a man, like me.'

EYEWITNESS - JIMMY ELLIS, 'It was a right to my chin in the fourth round that did the damage. I saw the left hands, but he sneaked up on me with the right and it ruined me. It hurt so bad I couldn't really fight my best after that. You would have thought that after all the rounds I've boxed with Muhammad I'd know about the right. But it took me by surprise.'

WHATEVER HAPPENED TO JIMMY ELLIS? After eight consecutive stoppage victories, Ellis was blasted out in the first round by Earnie Shavers in 1973, and he won just two of his final eight fights after that setback. His career ended when he suffered a detached retina after a sparring partner accidentally poked him in his left eye in 1975. Ali continued to employ father-of-six Jimmy as a sparring partner, but did not hit to the head. Ellis was appointed coach at the Muhammad Ali Boxing Club in Santa Monica, and he and his wife sang with a Baptist spiritual choir. As he approached his 70s Jimmy was diagnosed as suffering from dementia pugilistica, with no memory of his boxing career. He passed on in May 2014, aged 74.

Buster Mathis (USA)

**Venue: Houston, Texas
17 November 1971
Ali 227lb, Mathis 256lb
Ali WPTS12
(Ali purse: $300,000)**

THERE was more of Muhammad Ali than ever before when he returned to action four months later to put his NABF title on the line against Buster Mathis. He weighed in at 16st 3lb in old money, but was still dwarfed by the man mountain that was Mathis. Yet, despite the extra baggage, Muhammad moved with the old graceful speed and style that had become his trademark.

Mathis was one of the unlucky pieces in the jigsaw that linked the great boxers in this golden era for the heavyweight division. He had broken a hand winning the Olympic trials, and the man he beat in the final went to Tokyo and won the 1964 gold medal. His name: Joe Frazier.

A powerhouse puncher, Mathis was light on his feet for such a big man, but Ali found it easy to pick him off with his usual mix of flicking jabs and sudden bursts of combination punches.

Mathis stalked Ali with bravery and determination, occasionally trying to leap in with his lethal left hook that Ali avoided with his superbly timed head movements as he deliberately allowed the punches to whoosh past his chin. When one of the hooks bounced off the top of his head near the Mathis corner, Buster's second screamed, 'He's hurt, Buster. He's hurt!' Ali looked down at the trainer, winked and moved easily out of punching range.

Late in the 11th round Ali landed with a short, chopping right to the side of the jaw and Mathis fell on all fours, shaking the ring as his mighty frame hit the canvas. He was up at eight but on legs that were refusing to obey him. Ali unleashed a volley of punches, the last a right hand that landed on the top of Buster's head and knocked him to the floor again. It seemed to we onlookers that this combination was thrown almost reluctantly, none of the punches fired with real power.

Buster was still on the canvas as the bell rang with the count at four, and his cornermen hauled him back to his stool and got him ready for more punishment rather than do the humane thing and retire him.

He was sent out for the 12th and final round of a fight he had no hope of winning as we saw the unacceptable face of the merciless side of boxing. Ali had promised, 'This will be Buster's last stand. I will do to Buster what the Indians did to Custer. I'm gonna wipe him out.' But he had no appetite to apply the finishing blows.

He held back as Mathis came out on legs that were still unsteady, and it took just a gentle right hand to the temple to send him back to the canvas.

Showing bravery beyond the call of duty, Mathis struggled to his feet and Ali flicked him lightly with the left hand as he staggered around the ring and another half-strength right sent him back down in an untidy heap. The broken giant hauled himself up once more and valiantly tried to return to the attack while Ali patted him even more gently with the left and did not attempt to throw the right. In Ali's corner Angelo Dundee was yelling, 'Take him out, damn it, Ali! Take him out.'

But Ali purposely held off and allowed Mathis to finish on his feet, way behind on all three scorecards: Referee Chris Jordan 118-105, judge Ernie Taylor 118-104, judge Earl Keel 119-108.

BUSTER MATHIS

ALI AFTER-FIGHT QUOTE, 'I got to sleep good at night. How am I goin' to sleep if I just killed a man in front of his wife and son just to satisfy you writers? I held off because I don't want to be a killer in the ring. I shouldn't really be in this business. I don't have or want the killer instinct [deliberate pause]. Mind you, I'd find it for Frazier. I'll take him out and then retire to follow the wishes of Allah.'

EYEWITNESS – BUSTER MATHIS, 'Nobody can call me a dog anymore, I gave it all I had. It was exhaustion as much as anything that beat me tonight. I just had nothing left. I know I can fight and someday I'm gonna be the champion.'

WHATEVER HAPPENED TO BUSTER MATHIS? There was a tragic downhill run for Buster following his retirement in 1972 after a second-round defeat by Ron Lyle. He ballooned up to 36 stone because of an eating disorder and was a housebound invalid when he died of a heart attack at the age of 52 in 1995, two months before his son Buster Mathis Jnr was knocked out in two rounds by Mike Tyson in a non-title fight. Buster Snr's ring record: Fights 34, won 30 (21 inside the distance), lost four.

Jurgen Blin (Germany)

Venue: Zurich
26 December 1967
Ali 220lb, Blin 198lb
Ali WKO7
(Ali purse: $250,000)

ALI set off on the equivalent of what was famously labelled the Joe Louis Bum-A-Month Campaign, and his first port of call was Zurich in Switzerland and a fight with former German champion Jurgen Blin, who had few qualifications to be in the same ring as the man who continued to call himself The Greatest.

The 28-year-old, fair-haired Blin was approaching the end of his career and had a record of 29-8-6. He was noted for his stamina rather than his power, and had been stopped only once. Ali predicted that Blin would fall in the first round, but was persuaded by the promoters not to repeat the forecast because they needed to sell tickets for a fight that was staged, suitably, on Boxing Day. They managed to attract 7,000 fans, which meant the promotion made a financial loss after Ali had taken his guaranteed $250,000, with $45,000 going into the German's pocket.

Blin, a former slaughterman and butcher, somehow managed to write an entire book about the fight, which left his ghostwriter with more work to do than Jurgen managed in the ring. He huffed and puffed but could not get near stopping Ali, as he had boldly predicted before the fight. His best successes came in the early rounds when he landed with a ratio of one in five of the punches he was hurling at his elusive rival, who was showboating and introducing the Ali shuffle in Switzerland for the first time.

Ali was at his most mischievous and cocky, making the wildly aggressive Blin look a clown at times as his head-down, swinging attacks put the corner posts in more danger than an opponent performing his now-you-see-me-now-you-don't dancing tricks.

Following Angelo Dundee's instructions to start taking the fight seriously, Ali stopped dancing in the sixth round and jolted Blin with a series of solid head punches that at one stage almost knocked the game German out of the ring. You could not question Blin's courage, but you could question his tactics that too often played into the hands of the swaggering, supremely confident Kentuckian. It was completely one-sided, but Blin kept himself in with a chance of causing a major upset because of his giant heart and determination. He chased Ali around the ring swinging hopefully, but most of his punches punished thin air.

Ali decided to stop the exhibition boxing and stepped on the gas in the seventh round. A right uppercut pulled Blin up in his tracks, a following left hook and thumping right cross sent the German collapsing back against the ropes, and as he slithered to the canvas almost in slow motion referee Sepp Suter went through the formality of the ten-second count.

Ali had won without really breaking sweat, and he got a huge reception from the Swiss crowd as if he was the home hero.

ALI AFTER-FIGHT QUOTE, 'Nobody's ever knocked Blin out before, so it shows I am punching with the sort of power that will make Joe Frazier worry about me being back on his trail. Blin can be proud of his performance. He never stopped coming forward and gave it everything. But I knew I could take him whenever I chose the moment. I've had a wonderful welcome here in

Switzerland and I hope I gave them the entertainment they were hoping for.'

EYEWITNESS – JURGEN BLIN, 'It was an honour to be in the same ring as the greatest heavyweight of all time. There were several times when I had him concerned but he was too clever for me when I tried to get my strongest punches home. Deep in my heart I knew I had no chance of beating him. He was very generous with his praise of my performance at the end, and I will treasure the memory of having fought him. He knows he has been in a fight.'

WHATEVER HAPPENED TO JURGEN BLIN? Two defeats by Joe Bugner, including losing the European title he had taken from Jose Urtain, convinced Jurgen he should hang up his gloves in 1973. He had some rollercoaster adventures in the business world before going bankrupt. He later opened a successful pub in a corner of Hamburg's main railway station. It was announced on nationwide German television that he had committed suicide when in fact it was his boxer son, Knut, who took his own life after getting involved with an extreme religious sect. Jurgen's ring record: Fights 48, won 30 (eight inside the distance), lost 12, drew six.

Mac Foster (USA)

Venue: Tokyo
1 April 1972
Ali 226lb, Foster 212lb
Ali WPTS15
(Ali purse: $200,000)

HAVE-GLOVES-WILL-TRAVEL Muhammad Ali next arrived in Tokyo on his mission to get Joe Frazier back in the ring. Waiting for him in the opposite corner was powerfully built, 6ft 2in Vietnam War veteran Mac Foster, from Fresno, California, ranked ninth in the world and certainly not belonging in the 'bum' category. It was the first fight ever staged in Asia between two top-ten ranked heavyweights.

Ali treated the adoring Japanese public to every trick in his publicity book: refereed contests between Japanese pee-wee boxers, prayed at the Tokyo-Islamic temple, visited a US Air Force base, got 'knocked out' by his middleweight sparring partner for the benefit of the cameras, and signed hundreds of autographs after every training session. And, of course, he didn't stop talking and included this pre-fight prediction:

'Round five. It shall be over not in round four or six but round five. I like the number five. I get up at five in the morning and I run five miles. I eat five poached eggs for breakfast. I drink five glasses of orange juice and five glasses of ice water during the day. I take a nap at 5pm. My daughter is five years old. I have been married five years and I met my wife on the fifth day of the fifth month of the year.'

Mac Foster, son of Mississippi sharecroppers, the third of 11 children, could not get a word in. Nicknamed 'Mac the Knife', he turned down a university track and field scholarship to join the US Marines, won all the major services titles and went into this fight with only one defeat in 29 contests, a six-round stoppage by Jerry Quarry two years earlier. The Japanese promoters, still billing Ali as Cassius Clay, insisted on a 15-round championship distance, declaring, 'Clay is still the peoples' champion.'

To suit the television schedules in the USA, the fight started just after noon, or High Noon as the publicists tried to sell it.

Wearing a spectacular Japanese gown, Ali entered the ring carrying a pole with the number card for round five. The 15,000 crowd in the octagon-shaped Nihon Budokan (Martial Arts Hall) roared with excitement. But from the moment the first bell rang it was all less entertaining. A strangely lethargic Ali and an uncharacteristically cautious Mac Foster waltzed rather than raced through 15 undistinguished rounds.

Ali showed real urgency only in round five, firing a series of looping lefts and rights, trying to flatten Foster as he had predicted. But Mac the Knife withdrew into safe harbour behind a high defence and at the end of the round Ali looked deflated as the crowd jeered him back to his corner. It was April Fool's Day, and it was Ali who felt the fool.

This was one of Ali's most uneventful fights. He leant on the ropes in the seventh round, inviting Foster to take free pot shots at his body, the first unveiling of his rope-a-dope tactics, but the Californian could make little impression despite landing with a dozen short piston shots to the body. Ali's left jabs were rarely out of Foster's face and at the end of a generally tedious contest he was clearly ahead on all scorecards: Referee John Crowder 73-65, judge Takeo Ugo 75-67, judge Hiroyuki Tezaki 74-66.

Twelve-year-old Cassius Marcellus Clay, with all his jabbin' and gabbin' ahead of him

Golden Boy: Cassius Clay top of the world on the Olympic podium at the 1960 Rome Games

The first professional fight and Tunney Hunsaker bulldozes in against the slim-line local hero in Louisville

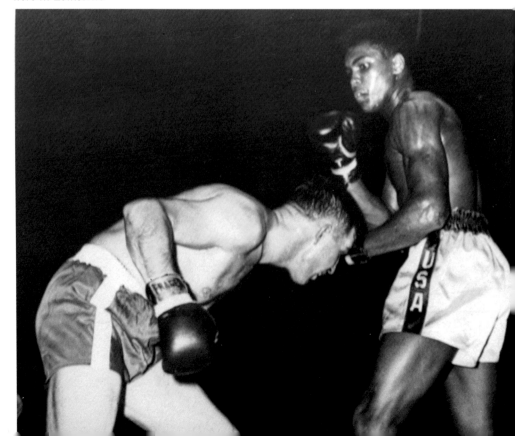

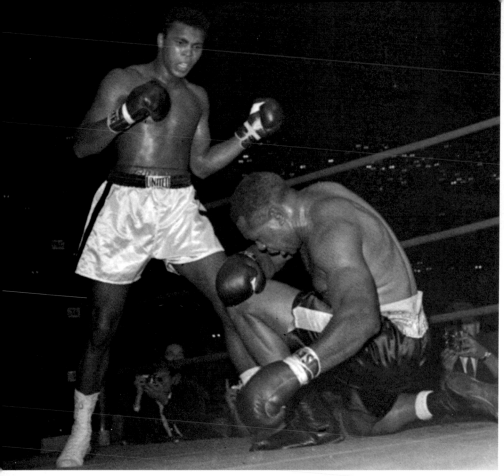

Ageless Archie Moore hits the floor in four, just as punching poet Clay prophesied

'Enery's 'Ammer has landed and Clay hits the deck in round four of his first fight against Henry Cooper

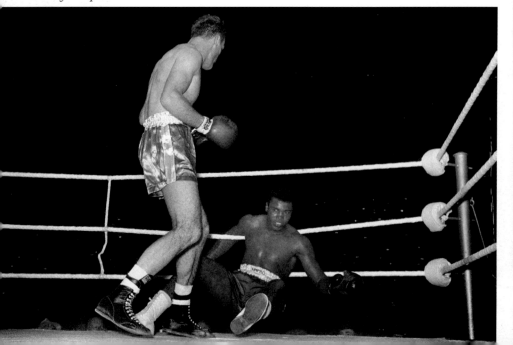

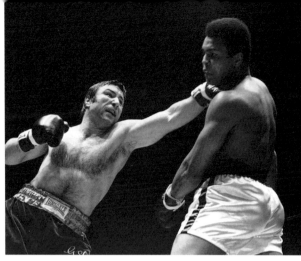

'I shook up the world!' Clay has just taken the title from 'Big Bad Bear' Sonny Liston

Forced to fight outside the USA after his refusal to join the Army, the now Muhammad Ali had his hands full with George Chuvalo in Toronto in 1966

Floyd Patterson tries to keep his head as Ali pounds him to defeat in the first of their two one-sided fights

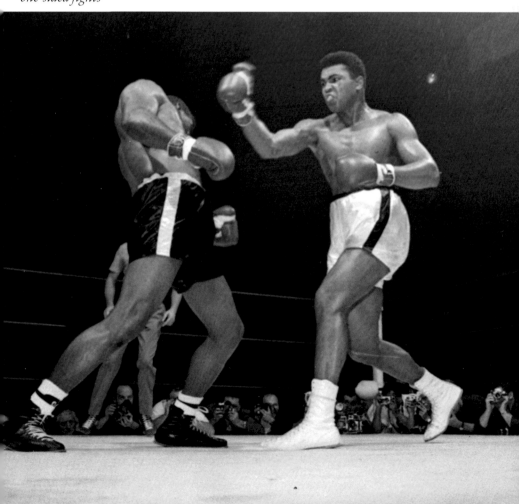

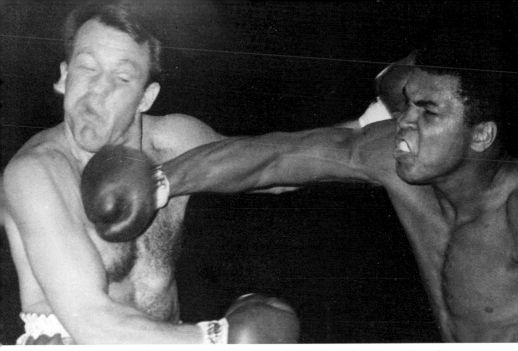

London blitzed. Ali thunders in a right cross on his way to a third round knockout win over Britain's Brian London

A bird's eye view of the climax of Ali's dismantling of Cleveland Williams in three rounds in Houston in 1966

At his cruellest, Ali demands of outgunned Ernie Terrell: 'What's ma name?'

This is a rarity, Ali ducking below the waist as he battles with British-Hungarian Joe Bugner in their first fight

Ali in snarling mood as he powers to an avenging win over Ken Norton in their second fight in California in 1973

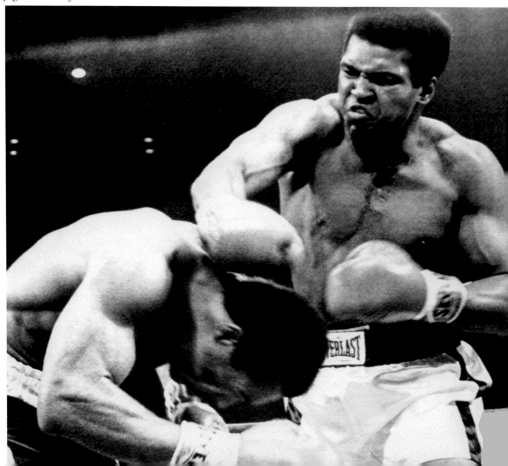

Jerry Quarry feels the power that gave Ali two stoppage victories over the big-hitting Californian

The Rumble in the Jungle ends with George Foreman spinning to a shock knockout defeat in the eighth round

This is the knockdown Ali always denied. He said it was a trip, but Chuck 'Rocky' Wepner insists it was caused by a clean punch

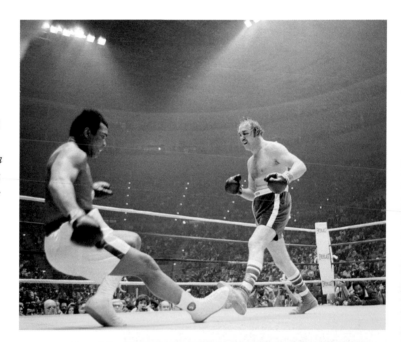

Ali lands a right cross during the bruising Thrilla in Manila in which he and Joe Frazier took each other 'to the edge of death'

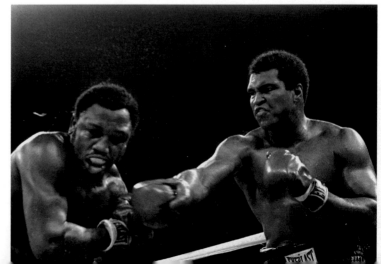

The final knockdown scored by Ali, and it's British bulldog Richard Dunn on the canvas in the fifth round of their world title fight in Munich in 1976

Only Ali would clown with the hardest hitting of all heavyweights as he polishes the bald head of Earnie Shavers on the way to a points victory

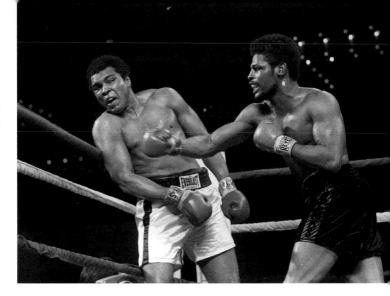

One of the shocks of the century as Ali loses his world title to the virtual novice Leon 'Neon' Spinks, but he regained his crown in the return match

Larry Holmes traps Ali in a corner on his way to forcing a surrender at the end of ten depressing rounds

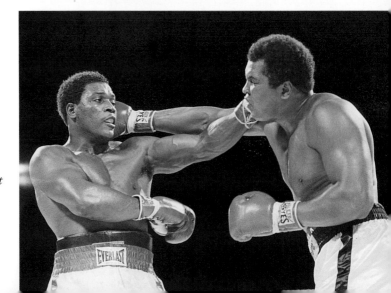

Ali's last stand, beaten on points in the Bahamas by Trevor Berbick. The curtain was about to come down on The Greatest.

MAC FOSTER

ALI AFTER-FIGHT QUOTE, 'I congratulated Foster at the end on his performance. He put up a good defence that made it difficult for me to get through with my best punches. We created history by fighting each other in Asia but the fact that we started at noon to suit TV at home left us both feeling a little sluggish. But I am one more victory and one more fight nearer getting Frazier back in the ring. The traps are set.'

EYEWITNESS – MAC FOSTER, 'My plan was to conserve my energy until the second half of the fight. I had never been past eight rounds before, and 15 rounds seemed like a marathon. When I tried to increase the pressure in the last third of the fight I found I had little in the tank and just had to fight for survival.'

WHATEVER HAPPENED TO MAC FOSTER? Foster retired from boxing in 1976 after losing his fourth consecutive decision, this time to raw prospect Stan Ward. His final record was 30-6, with all 30 of his wins coming on stoppages. He was a prominent youth boxing coach until becoming affected by an MRSA infection and he died following heart complications on 19 July 2010. He was 68. A cheerful and likeable man, Mac was survived by his wife Yolanda and their four children.

George Chuvalo (Canada)

Venue: Vancouver
1 May 1972
Ali 217lb, Chuvalo 221lb
Ali WPTS12
(Ali purse: $200,000)

ALI returned to Canada on May Day 1972 for what he described as unfinished business. He was bravely going back into a minefield to face George Chuvalo, the opponent he had described as 'the hardest man on the planet' after their first fight in Toronto in 1966, when he had been dragged into a war before winning on points over 15 punishing rounds.

As part of the ticket-selling spiel, Ali said that he had not completed the job the first time around, and that this time he would become the first fighter ever to knock Chuvalo off his feet. He put up his NABF title as incentive for the Canadian, who since their last meeting had won 32 of 37 fights. Two of his defeats – by Joe Frazier and George Foreman – had been stoppages, but neither had been able to knock him down.

Ali fed on this to get bums on seats. 'I'm not gonna let it be said there was ever a heavyweight that didn't fall,' he said. 'They have pictures showing my heels in the air. Jack Johnson fell, Jack Dempsey fell, Joe Louis fell, Rocky Marciano fell, Joe Frazier fell, and George Chuvalo is sure as hell gonna fall.' Chuvalo countered: 'Ali is still talking a great fight, but he's not as good as he was at putting action to go with his words. The fact is I'm a better fighter than I was in 1966 and he's not as good a fighter as he was since his long lay-off. You can almost hear the rust in his bones. I only had three weeks to prepare when we first met. This time I am as fit as can be and am ready to get my revenge.'

Any ideas Ali had of flooring Chuvalo probably disappeared in the first round when a right uppercut landed flush on the Canuck's craggy chin. It would have knocked most opponents cold. Chuvalo barely blinked and walked forward throwing his 'washerwoman' combination punches.

Ali wisely decided to concentrate on collecting points with a left jab that was hardly out of Chuvalo's face. The crude but courageous Canadian rocked Ali with a heavy right cross in round five, and Muhammad retreated to the ropes and leant back, daring Chuvalo to hit him. George thrashed away with both fists, but made no impact against a mocking opponent.

In the sixth round Ali went all out to knock Chuvalo off his feet. He let fly with every shot in his arsenal, jolting George with a series of combinations, but the 'Croatian Rock' just shrugged off the punches and the pain and kept on coming forward into the hail of leather.

From then on Ali settled for a distance battle, and kept picking Chuvalo off with accurate jabs to clinch a unanimous points decision: Referee Dave Brown 59-51, judge Tommy Paonessa 60-46, judge Tommy Keyes 58-51.

For George there was the satisfaction of once again not visiting the canvas. In 93 professionals fights, he was never knocked off his feet. He was a remarkably tough and often foolishly brave fighter, who never knew the meaning of retreat.

ALI AFTER-FIGHT QUOTE, 'I'm tired of hitting George. He eats punches like other people eat burgers. I landed punches in there that would have knocked out most fighters. He just shrugged and kept coming forward. I don't know of anybody harder. He is armour-plated. I'm getting closer to Joe Frazier and when I get him back in the ring I'm gonna amaze ya.'

EYEWITNESS - GEORGE CHUVALO, 'Ali was not as fast as he used to be, but he is punching harder. There were a few times in there tonight when I had him hanging on, but he's still got great defensive skill and I could not land major punches when I needed to. That's 25 rounds I've gone with The Greatest and I've looked him in the eye the whole way. I like the man and hope he gives me another shot when he gets the title back.'

WHATEVER HAPPENED TO GEORGE CHUVALO? George's life outside the ring had been scarred with tragedy. He lost one son to suicide and two others to drug overdoses, and his wife in a fit of depression took her own life. George remarried and he and his second wife, Joanne, toured high schools speaking about the futility of drug use. Chuvalo's ring accomplishments were recognized when he was inducted into the Canadian and World Boxing Halls of Fame, and he was honoured with the Order of Canada in 1998. His ring record: Fights 93, wins 73 (64 inside the distance), lost 18, drew two. Idolised in the European country of his parents' birth, a statue of George in fighting pose has been erected in Herzegovina.

Jerry Quarry (USA)

**Venue: Las Vegas
27 June 1972
Ali 216lb, Quarry 198lb
Ali WRSF7
(Ali purse: $500,000)**

PROMOTER Don King, larger than life and even more verbose and vociferous than Muhammad Ali, made a lot of noise about the double header that he staged at the Convention Center in Las Vegas, featuring Ali in a return with Jerry Quarry and Bob Foster defending his world light-heavyweight title against Jerry's younger brother, Mike Quarry. King billed it as 'The Soul Brothers vs. The Quarry Brothers', and this brought accusations of the two fights carrying racial undertones.

It was a bad night for the Quarrys. Jerry had to go into the ring to face Ali after watching Mike knocked cold by a Bob Foster left hook that stretched him flat out on the canvas for five minutes while getting urgent medical attention.

This was hardly the best preparation for a fight in which Jerry vowed to get revenge for his third-round cut-eye defeat in Ali's first comeback fight after his three-and-a-half-year exile.

Ali also watched the Foster victory on a TV screen in his dressing room, and said, 'One White Hope down, one to go. Tell everybody to take their seats in all the theatres across the nation to see another annihilation.'

Quarry, who had talked a good fight in response to Ali's usual taunts, tried to intimidate Ali by lifting him off the canvas in an early clinch. It was a moment of bravado for which he paid a painful price. Ali toyed with him for six one-sided rounds, punishing him with streams of left jabs and long, jolting rights that had Quarry's head going back on his shoulders like a punch ball.

This was Ali at his most arrogant and invincible. He was supremely confident, and held conversations with ringside reporters during the interval of each round. As he went out for the start of the seventh round, he shouted down to co-commentators Eamonn Andrews and Reg Gutteridge, 'Time to go to work.'

He blasted Quarry with a flurry of lefts and rights while inviting referee Mike Kaplan to step in. A huge right uppercut rocked Irish Jerry back on his heels and this time Kaplan followed Ali's instructions and waved the one-sided fight over.

There was chaos in the ring at the finish, with Ali being interviewed by a scrum of television reporters who were fighting with each other to get their microphones to Ali's face. Then, while giving an interview that was being broadcast to the crowd, Ali spotted George Foreman at ringside and started to challenge him. 'Frazier's getting in the ring with you rather than me 'cos he knows you're easy,' he yelled. 'Frazier is hiding from me. Why don't you fight the real champion? Frazier's just borrowing my title.'

As Foreman shouted back, Ali leant over the ropes and hit him in the face with a fierce left jab. 'That's just a taste of what's to come,' said Ali. 'Come to my dressing room and we'll have it on right now.'

ALI AFTER-FIGHT QUOTE, 'I carried Quarry because I needed the rounds, and also because I wanted to make sure he was completely demoralised before I finished him off. Joe Frazier's still running away from me. He's taking an easy defence against George Foreman rather than get back in the ring with me. He can't keep running away from me. I'll catch up with him and get my title back.'

EYEWITNESS - JERRY QUARRY, 'I could have carried on. The referee let Ali referee the fight. I still had lots of bombs to throw. I started slow because I was in shock over what happened to my brother. That really shook me up, seeing him taken out by that Foster punch. It meant I was not as focused as I should have been against Ali.'

WHATEVER HAPPENED TO JERRY QUARRY? Quarry paid the price for being a goalkeeper of a boxer, stopping everything with his face. He became a tragic figure, dying in a punch-drunk condition in 1999 at the age of 53. Jerry earned more than $2m as a top contender in the 1960s and 70s but was reduced to living on social security at the end and was unaware of his own name. It was a degrading fall for a man who had been considered one of the most intelligent and insightful television boxing pundits. He finished his pro career with a 53-9-4 record after having fought more than 200 bouts as an amateur. Seven years later Mike Quarry also died from the effects of pugilistic dementia, and another Quarry boxing brother suffered Ali-style Parkinson's disease. The Quarrys gave their all to the unforgiving sport of boxing.

Alvin 'Blue' Lewis (USA)

Venue: Croke Park, Dublin
19 July 1972
Ali 217lb, Lewis 223lb
Ali WRSF11
(Ali purse: $200,000)

E VEN by Muhammad Ali's standards, his 39th professional fight was extraordinary and bordering on the unbelievable. It was put together by a Kerry-born circus strongman, and coming from the opposite corner to Ali was a convicted killer. Some would say it could only have happened in Ireland, and Ali won the hearts of a nation as he played on his Irish ancestry. Just to add to the Irishness of it all, it was a fight that Ali won twice.

If you ever get the chance, watch the award-winning documentary on the fight: *When Ali Came to Ireland*, lovingly produced by Ross Whitaker and Aideen O'Sullivan. It not only tells the story of the fight, but the fascinating background facts of how circus performer and publican Michael 'Butty' Sugrue put up £300,000 that he did not have and persuaded Ali to 'come home to Ireland' to fight against Alvin 'Blue' Lewis in Croke Park in the summer of 1972.

Lewis was a former Ali sparring partner, who had done a long stretch for manslaughter in his home state of Michigan. He was rewarded with this fight for his loyalty to Muhammad during his bitter battle with the United States establishment.

The fight lost a small fortune because many of the 25,000 spectators gatecrashed and watched for nothing. Ali got his guaranteed $200,000 and Lewis his $35,000, but the local banks had not recouped their investment when Sugrue passed away in 1977.

Ali, suffering from a heavy head cold, was happy to treat the fight as little more than a sparring exhibition until Lewis got ambitious in the fifth round and launched a powerful two-fisted attack. It shook Ali out of his lethargy and he released a blistering burst of punches, ending with a vicious right that dropped Lewis flat on his back and seemingly out for the count.

American referee Lew Eskin could not pick up the timekeeper's count and was at least five seconds behind him and had reached nine when the bell rang. Angelo Dundee insisted that it was a 22-second count!

From then on Ali virtually carried the outclassed Lewis without ever really getting into top gear. He totally dominated exchanges until the 11th when Eskin decided Lewis had eaten enough of Ali's left jabs and waved the fight over. Affable Al responded by lifting Ali up in the air as if he was a trophy. It was the strangest reaction from any of Ali's beaten opponents.

The fans were in an Ali frenzy and so many invaded the ring it was in danger of collapsing. It took Ali 30 minutes to battle his way through the crowd back to his dressing room. Promoter Sugrue helped beat a path for him, using the strength that he showed when pulling tractors along with his teeth. It was wonderful madness.

With good local blarney, it was suggested Muhammad change his name again to O'Ali in recognition of his paternal great-grandfather, an Irish-born white slave owner. As a recent convert to the Nation of Islam, it could be said that Ali had mixed feelings about his white Irish heritage.

ALI AFTER-FIGHT QUOTE, 'I have never had a warmer welcome in my life than here in Ireland. I felt my Irish ancestors dancing deep inside me. That's the first time I've beaten anybody twice in the same fight. Al was knocked out in the fifth. I thought the referee was counting sheep. This was a good warm-up for my next fight against Floyd Patterson on my way towards regaining my title.'

EYEWITNESS – AL LEWIS, 'I want to thank Ali for allowing me to share the same ring as him. He is a special fighter and a special man. The Irish fans were incredible. They treated me like a hero, and appreciated that I did my best against the man who quite rightly calls himself The Greatest. I had no idea what was going on in that fifth round, but just knew the ref had not called ten and out.'

WHATEVER HAPPENED TO AL LEWIS? Lewis won three fights against little-known opponents after losing to Ali before his career was freakishly brought to an end in November 1973. He was playing the Good Samaritan when he stopped to help a priest whose car had broken down. When he lifted the bonnet to look at the engine the battery sparked, spitting acid in an eye and causing enough damage to get his boxing licence revoked. His final ring record: Fights 36, won 30 (19 inside the distance), lost six.

Floyd Patterson (USA)

Venue: Madison Square Garden, NY
29 September 1972
Ali 218lb, Patterson 188lb
Ali WRSF7
(Ali purse: $250,000)

IN contrast to the bitterness of their first fight in 1965, Muhammad Ali held out an olive branch of peace to Floyd Patterson before their return match in Floyd's hometown of New York. Ali decided to be respectful, and took every opportunity to praise Patterson's distinguished contribution to boxing. It was almost as if he was preparing a eulogy for the man who had been world heavyweight champion when he first started making a name for himself as Cassius Clay.

Patterson, now 37, was motivated by thoughts of revenge for the humiliating defeat by the then young, loud-mouthed braggart in Las Vegas seven years earlier. The prospect of a more even fight drew a crowd to the Garden of 17,378 – many of them stars from stage, screen, television and Wall Street. They say the fight emptied Broadway, both the theatre seats and the stage. Ali was the biggest show in town.

He began the evening with some Broadway-style theatrics when Joe Frazier entered the ring, introduced as 'the only man to beat

Ali'. Gesturing, pulling faces and throwing punches, he pretended to go after Frazier. 'Bundini, stop holdin' me back, let me at him!' he shouted. It was clowning with an undercurrent of menace.

Patterson clearly had a plan of campaign to ensure he performed better than in Vegas, and after chasing Ali's shadow in the opening stages, he won the third, fourth and fifth rounds, mainly because of Ali's showboating, but also because Floyd was finding the target with smart combination punches.

Responding to the nagging from Angelo Dundee in the corner, Ali stopped being flippant and casual and opened up the sixth round with serious intent. He unleashed a furious flurry of uppercuts and slashing rights, one of which opened a cut on Patterson's left eyelid.

Again in the seventh, with Patterson's eye closing rapidly, Ali continued the assault, deliberately targeting the eye, which by now was shut tight like an oyster shell.

As the bell rang for the start of round eight, Patterson – never ever a quitter – got off his stool like the born warrior that he was to continue to fight. But with good sense, the doctor had advised the referee Arthur Mercante to stop the contest, and he waved it over.

There were undeserved boos from the crowd, and a compassionate and considerate Ali grabbed the ring microphone to proclaim the virtues of Floyd Patterson.

It was the end of an era and Floyd never fought again.

ALI AFTER-FIGHT QUOTE, 'Floyd Patterson was my idol when I first came into boxing. He is a great, great fighter. I thought he'd be nothing tonight, but he surprised me and gave me a hard contest. I didn't knock him out. I didn't get him on a TKO. All I did was close his eye. He has not been given the credit he deserves for the way he has represented our sport. He is a gentleman, a sportsman, a very proud man and one helluva fighter.'

EYEWITNESS - FLOYD PATTERSON, 'I would have fought on. As long as I had one good eye, I felt I had a chance. I did better this time than in the first fight, when I was handicapped by a back injury. My problem tonight was I just couldn't see his right hand coming throughout the seventh round. I insisted I wanted to fight on, but the doctor told the referee he should stop it. I did not retire. I wanted to go out on my shield. Now I will take some time out while I think what I want to do next. Boxing is and always will be my life.'

WHATEVER HAPPENED TO FLOYD PATTERSON? There was no announcement of Floyd's retirement, but he never stepped back into the ring. He continued his close links with boxing and became the highly respected chairman of the New York State Athletic Commission, and was inducted into the International Boxing Hall Of Fame. His three-fight rivalry with Ingemar Johansson developed into a close friendship, and he regularly visited Ingo in Sweden and they ran the 1982 and 1983 Stockholm marathons together.

He trained his adopted son, Tracy Harris Patterson, who became a world super-featherweight champion in the 1990s. In later life Floyd suffered from Alzheimer's, caused by taking too many punches, and he also had prostate cancer and died at home in New York in 2006, aged 71. He will be remembered as a true gentleman of the ring. His final ring record: Fights 64, won 55 (40 inside the distance), eight losses and one draw.

Bob Foster (USA)

Venue: Lake Tahoe, Nevada
21 November 1972
Ali 221lb, Foster 180lb
Ali WKO8
(Ali purse: $260,000)

THE promoters had to use their imagination and fire up their PR engine to full power to try to convince the public that world light-heavyweight champion Bob Foster had a hope of beating Muhammad Ali in the thin air of Lake Tahoe, the little cousin of Las Vegas. For starters, they claimed the 6,200-foot altitude in Tahoe would exhaust Ali but favour Foster, who away from the ring was a deputy sheriff in Albuquerque (4,943 feet).

They pointed out that Foster had once beaten Ali when they were amateurs, and that he was now quicker, taller, and faster than Ali and had a left hook that was harder than any punch in Muhammad's armoury. Perhaps conveniently, they played down the fact that Foster would be giving away more than 40 pounds, and that Joe Frazier had wiped him out in two savage rounds.

Ali predicted Foster would fall in five, and the promoters countered that by calling in comedy actor Bill Cosby to root for Foster. 'If Foster lands with his left hook, it will be goodnight Ali,' said Cosby, who then helped the publicity by getting into the ring and joke-sparring with Ali, and pointing out that he was fat. 'You're right,' said Ali. 'Maybe it's time I gave up fighting and got myself a soft job in the movies.'

The unlikely setting for the fight was a nightclub in a gambling casino. At a press conference, Ali was asked how he as a teetotal Muslim minister could walk between slot machines and dice tables and waitresses in orange boots to get to and from his training ring. Bundini Brown jumped in with the answer, 'The champ don't care about this stuff. He just goes right through it without seeing it.'

As the fight started in a sparkling red, white and blue ring set up on the nightclub floor, waiters moved among the booths and tables serving drinks. Ali clowned through the first two rounds, using his extra weight to push Foster around, patting him on the head and pawing him like a bear. He was overdoing the clowning and some of the gamblers began booing. One loudly shouted, 'Phony!'

Bundini yelled, 'Stop playing with him, champ!' Turning sideways and completely ignoring the stalking Foster, Ali looked at Bundini and ordered, 'Shut up.'

In the fourth round Foster landed with a right that raised a purple mouse under Ali's left eye, but Ali was holding back until the fifth when he came out with serious intent, determined to make his prediction come true. His punches, pawed up until now, suddenly carried his full weight and Foster crumbled under a vicious two-fisted assault. The world light-heavyweight champion was up and down like a yo-yo, taking four counts. But Ali, bleeding from a small cut beneath his left eyebrow, could not finish his opponent off in the predicted round, which brought derisive catcalls from liberally lubricated spectators.

Ali danced and kept his distance as he protected his eye in the sixth, knocked Foster down twice more in the seventh, and then appeared shaken by desperate right hands from Foster, who was still dangerous like a wounded tiger. But after 40 seconds of the eighth round, Ali took careful aim and found the lawman's jaw. Down went the sheriff for a seventh time, and this time he failed to beat the count. Ali hugged him as he struggled to his feet. The gamblers cheered and then returned to the tables and their own personal wars against the odds.

ALI AFTER-FIGHT QUOTE, 'When Foster cut me I knew I had to get to work. I don't want anybody messing with my pretty face. He was always dangerous because he has the punch of a mule and takes out most of his opponents with a single punch. But he's never met anybody with a chin as strong as mine. Frazier's looking for an easy life, taking that Foreman fight. He knows I'm gonna whup him, then I'll have a couple of defences and then maybe go into the movies. The camera will just love me.'

EYEWITNESS – BOB FOSTER, 'Ali wobbled when I hit him and he wasn't fooling, I hurt him. He can't punch hard enough to knock out Joe Frazier. He'll never beat him. Ali hurt me with shots I couldn't see. He's got a trick. He jabs and covers your eye with his thumb. When he comes off the jab, he hits you with a right that you can't see. It's a good trick. But I could have beaten him if I'd used my left hand more, and if I'd been a little heavier.'

WHATEVER HAPPENED TO BOB FOSTER? Winning seven of his last ten fights, Foster retired in 1978 with his reputation intact as being one of the greatest light-heavyweights of all time. He returned to his police work in Albuquerque, and became a detective. Bob was inducted into the International Boxing Hall of Fame in 1990, and kept his interest in boxing as a trainer. His ring record: Fights 65, wins 56 (46 inside the distance), eight losses and one draw.

Joe Bugner (UK)

**Venue: Las Vegas
14 February 1973
Ali 217lb, Bugner 219lb
Ali WPTS12
(Ali purse: $285,000)**

THE boxing world was still in a state of shock over the ease with which George Foreman had relieved Joe Frazier of the world heavyweight title when Ali took on Britain's enigmatic Joe Bugner at the Convention Center in Las Vegas. Frazier had been blasted out in two wild rounds in Jamaica 23 days earlier. Suddenly Ali's contest with European champion Bugner took on new significance, and he now had Foreman as well as Frazier in his sights.

To sell seats, Ali talked of a Valentine's Day massacre. He predicted a seventh-round knockout win against the 6ft 4in Hungarian-born Bugner, who in 1971 managed to make himself unpopular in his adopted country by relieving national treasure Henry Cooper of his titles with a hugely controversial points victory. Joe had since been outpointed by Jack Bodell and undistinguished American Larry Middleton, but had redeemed himself by ripping the European crown from Jurgen Blin with an impressive eight-round knockout victory.

It was cruelly said of Bugner that he was built like a Greek statue but was less mobile. Big Joe, still only 22, shrugged off the sneers and was about to prove that he was comfortable in the company of the man continuing to call himself The Greatest.

Ali entered the ring wearing a stunning jewel-studded robe bearing the inscription on the back, 'People's Champion'. It was a gift from Elvis Presley, and Bugner was soon looking all shook up when a first-round combination of punches opened a nasty cut over his left eye.

It was a huge handicap for Bugner, and he was forced to box even more cautiously than usual, which meant defence was his main preoccupation.

We regular Ali watchers realised we would no longer see the twinkle-toed dancing entertainer from back in his Clay days. He was now a master of conserving his energy, fighting much of the time on flat feet and content to rest on the ropes, mixing in just occasional up-on-his-toes footwork of old.

Against Bugner, he concentrated on doing just enough to dictate without ever looking devastating.

There was not the usual frivolity stitched into Ali's work, and he settled for a distance fight after going flat out and failing to stop Bugner in the named seventh round. He let fly with a succession of hard-hitting attacks but found out why his young opponent was rated to have a strong chin, despite a knockout defeat in his professional debut as a 17-year-old rookie.

Bugner rarely made a fully committed offensive move, and often lay on the ropes Ali-style and took cover behind a fortress of a guard. His best shot was a right counter that occasionally took Ali by surprise and woke him up to the fact that he had a job to do.

At the end of 12 fairly pedestrian rounds all three judges scored it comfortably for Ali: Roland Dakin 57-54, Lou Tabat 56-53, Ralph Mosa 57-52.

ALI AFTER-FIGHT QUOTE, 'Bugner surprised me. He's got better legs than I thought. I won't be around in two years. Watch out for

Bugner. He'll be the champion a couple of years from now. I'll get out of boxing once I've finished my business with Joe Frazier and taken my title from Foreman. That will be Bugner's time, when I retire as undefeated champion.'

EYEWITNESS – JOE BUGNER, 'I've silenced those people who said I didn't deserve to be in the ring with Ali. They forget I sparred with him before his fight with Buster Mathis, so I knew a lot of his tricks. Apart from the cut eye in the first round, he gave me no real problems and I was always in the fight. If it had not been for the cut, I'd have given him a lot more trouble. I had to protect the eye and so was less aggressive than we'd planned. I'm still young and have plenty of time to improve. None of the world's leading heavyweights scare me.'

Bugner proved he was not just talk by giving Joe Frazier a hard contest in his next fight, closing the former world champion's eye and surviving a tenth-round knockdown before losing on points over 12 rounds at London's Earls Court. He was the only boxer to take on Ali and Frazier in back-to-back fights.

And a lucrative return with Ali was on the horizon. Not bad for the young man allegedly less mobile than a Greek statue.

Ken Norton (USA)

Venue: San Diego
31 March 1973
Ali 221lb, Norton 210lb
Ali LPTS12
(Ali purse: $210,000)

NOBODY knew exactly which punch from Ken Norton caused the damage, but from round one Muhammad Ali was complaining to cornerman Angelo Dundee that his jaw had been broken. He had gone into the fight in the clutches of complacency, dismissing Norton as 'an amateur'. The ex-Marine with the perfectly sculptured body literally shut the biggest mouth in sport, and caused one of the most unexpected upsets in heavyweight boxing history.

Looking on from ringside, not much seemed to happen in that first round, just the usual tentative feeling-out jabs from each fighter, a couple of crisp right hands by Norton. But there was nothing that appeared damaging.

At the bell Ali had blood on his mouth and he said to Dundee, 'I think I've got a broken jaw.'

Dundee said later, 'He must've gotten hit with his mouth open,' which was a reasonable assumption with chatterboxer Ali. As round two ended, another in which few power punches were landed,

Dundee asked the sluggish Ali, 'Do you want to quit?' Ali said no, despite being in considerable pain, and he started to box on his toes like the old-style Ali but against an opponent who was proving himself far from amateur status. He had lost only one of 31 fights, although fighting mostly second-rate opposition.

It was Norton, gaining in confidence with every round, who was doing the talking as the sixth round began. 'You're nothing,' he taunted, and landed his best punch yet, a hard, jarring right to Ali's head. Few of his opponents had seemed less intimidated.

Ali got back on his toes and danced, as we later found out because he did not want to risk taking any more punches on his aching jaw. He slowed Norton's advance with jolting jabs and once, as the eighth began, shook him with a short, vicious right.

Norton was crude in comparison to Ali and missed with more punches than he landed, but there was an eye-catching energy coming from him that the self-described Greatest seemed to lack. We got early signs of rope-a-dope from Ali as he leant back, inviting Norton to let go with winging blows to his midriff, and this tenth-round aggression helped swing the fight Norton's way. Once, as Ali forced his head down with his notorious holding tricks, Ken bent his knees and lifted him clear off the canvas. It was a staggering display of strength.

Ali was clearly tiring but rallied in the 11th round and had Norton covering up against a sustained attack during which his punches were sharper than at any other time in the fight.

As the last round was about to start, Norton's ring-wise trainer Eddie Futch told him, 'Win this one, Ken, and you've got the fight.' And that's exactly what he did. It was a split decision: Referee Frank Rustich 4-7, judge Hal Rickards 4-5, judge Fred Hayes 6-5.

A sad-looking Ali, whose cheek was swollen as a sign of the damage, was taken to hospital where the diagnosis was a broken jaw, which was wired during an operation and he could not open it properly for the next six weeks.

Plans for fights with Frazier and Foreman were put on hold. First, he had to try to avenge his defeat by Norton.

ALI AFTER-FIGHT QUOTE, 'I knew early on that my jaw had been broken. I was concentrating so hard on trying to beat Norton that I was not that aware of the pain. He was a far better fighter than I thought, and now I know I have to be in the best shape possible for our next fight. But I'm still after Frazier and Foreman. I've just been delayed.'

EYEWITNESS – KEN NORTON, 'I had been working on my confidence by having hypnosis, and I also got motivation from a book called *Think and Grow Rich*. My favourite part was a poem quoted in the book:

> Life's battles don't always go
> To the stronger or faster man
> But soon or late the man who wins
> Is the man who thinks he can

That convinced me I could beat Ali provided I had the right attitude. When he called me an amateur before the fight I smiled to myself. It proved to me that he was thinking he was in for an easy night. I knew otherwise. I'm happy to give him a return, and I will give him the same treatment.'

Ken Norton (USA)

Venue: Inglewood, California
10 September 1973
Ali 212lb, Norton 205lb
Ali WPTS12
(Ali purse: $535,000)

ONCE Ali's jaw was back in working order, he got himself in tip-top shape for the return with Norton, taking ten pounds off as he prepared to 'move and groove' against the man who had handed him the second defeat of his professional career. He usually spent a maximum of a month preparing for a fight. For this contest he worked in the training camp for 12 weeks, and promised to come into the ring 'with no flab, some gab and plenty of jab'.

Ali said he had come in at his 'dancin' weight' and moved at helter-skelter speed around the ring in the foundation stages, keeping Norton off balance with snapping left jabs and long overarm follow-through rights. To emphasise his super fitness to his opponent sitting in the opposite corner, he stood during the interval of the early rounds while listening to the words of wisdom from Angelo Dundee and the excited preaching of Bundini Brown.

To inspire his man, cheerleader Brown almost got on to the apron during the second round, shouting and screaming his support. Referee Dick Young warned him to shut up or leave the corner.

Late in the round the stalking Norton tested Ali's repaired jaw with a thumping left hook, but he gave no sign that it had bothered him.

As in the first fight, Norton lifted Ali off his feet as his counter to being pushed down at close quarters. He was showing that while Ali may be the fastest, he was the strongest. As well as a matter of muscle it was developing into a mind battle. Both were trying to psyche each other out.

Norton, attacking from behind a cross-armed guard, started to cut off Ali's path and he caught him in a neutral corner with a venomous right hand. This was just before the bell at the end of the fourth round and it was a psychological advantage to Norton when Ali slumped on his stool, abandoning his stand-up routine.

Becoming more aggressive as the fight wore on, Norton cut back Ali's early lead and pummelled the former world champion on the ropes in rounds ten and 11. Just as it looked as if Norton was taking complete control Ali produced a sweeping right uppercut that stopped Ken in his tracks and for a few seconds he appeared to be doing an unintended impersonation of the Ali shuffle.

Many good judges had them dead level going into the 12th and final round. This was when Ali reached down into his reserves of strength and stamina and produced his best round of the fight as he drove Norton around the ring with a blitz of two-fisted attacks. He put everything into it to the point that he was on the edge of exhaustion as the final bell signalled the end of an epic battle.

The over-enthusiastic Bundini Brown crowded in on him and he punched him out of the way in undisguised annoyance. Sometimes the clown could be a clot.

There was a lot of tension in the Ali corner before the announcement of a split-decision victory for Ali. Judge John Thomas scored it 6-5 for Ali, judge George Latka 5-6 for Norton, and referee Dick Young came down 7-5 on Ali's side. It was what Wellington would have called (after Waterloo) a damn close run thing.

ALI AFTER-FIGHT QUOTE, 'Ken Norton is the best opponent I have ever fought. No other man could hit me as much as he did in the shape I'm in. Frazier couldn't, Foreman wouldn't. I know it was close, that's why I finished fast just to remove any doubts about the winner. Maybe I overtrained for this one, and left some of me in the gym. I damaged my right hand in the sixth round, otherwise I would have won more clearly. I'm taking one more warm-up fight this year, then the traps will be set for Frazier and Foreman in that order.'

EYEWITNESS – KEN NORTON, 'I know I won this fight, just like I won the first time. Ali has to give me a rematch. It's one-one now, but I know in my heart it's really two-nothing to me. I'm grateful to Ali for helping me earn decent money at last. Before our first fight the most I'd ever earned was $8,000. My guarantee tonight was $200,000. It's made me hungry for more. Maybe I should get a shot at Foreman ahead of Ali. I deserve it.'

They say you should be careful what you wish for. Norton got his wish and challenged Foreman for the world title in his next fight in Caracas. Peak-power George smashed him to defeat in three rounds.

Rudi Lubbers (Holland)

Venue: Jakarta
20 October 1973
Ali 217lb, Lubbers 198lb
Ali WPTS12
(Ali purse: $200,000)

ALI got so bored during this virtual exhibition match against Dutch heavyweight champion Rudi Lubbers that he called British television commentator Reg Gutteridge up into his corner to give snatched inter-round interviews. He looked into the camera and apologised to his London fans for his performance. 'I'm getting old,' he said. 'I would have had this fight won in the first round when I was younger.'

Lubbers, stocky, thick-thighed and really a blown-up cruiserweight, had done little to justify being in the ring with The Master. He had won 20 fights against mediocre opposition before challenging for the European heavyweight title, when he was clearly outpointed by Joe Bugner at London's Albert Hall in January 1973. That convinced the Ali camp he was a safe opponent for what was a final warm-up for his return fight against Joe Frazier.

'Warm-up' proved a bit of an understatement. It was steaming hot in the Bung Kamo Stadium in Jakarta as Ali and Lubbers prepared to feature in the first 'live' satellite show from Indonesia of any kind.

There was huge, almost fanatical support for Ali wherever he went in Indonesia, which has a larger Muslim population than any other country in the world. He was mobbed at every mosque that he visited, and his training sessions drew the interest of thousands of spectators, many of them chanting his name. He was like a Pied Piper, followed by admiring children at every turn. It was true hero worship. They could have put him in the ring with a dummy and they would have pulled a huge crowd. Instead, they came up with a Dutchman who was little more than a sparring partner.

Ali went into the ring with a secret. The right fist he injured in the second fight with Ken Norton had still not mended, but he was confident he could beat Lubbers with one hand.

The contrast in physique of Ali and Lubbers was somewhat comical with the Dutchman having to almost jump to try to land head punches that were telegraphed and easily blocked.

Every round was virtually the same, Ali flicking with his left, feinting with his right and then an occasional Ali shuffle to keep the fans happy, while Lubbers walked stubbornly forward behind a high guard and throwing punches that invariably fell short of their target.

There was not a hint of a knockdown. Both fighters were affected by the severe heat and were happy to coast through much of the fight. Lubbers was there to survive, and Ali was there to entertain and take the money and run. It was a bit of a bank raid, really.

After the 12 uneventful rounds, Ali was awarded a clear-cut unanimous points decision. It was one of his least memorable fights.

ALI AFTER-FIGHT QUOTE, 'I wish I could have put on a better show, but I had to protect my right hand and so just concentrated on using my left. I'm saving my right for Joe Frazier. I'll take away happy memories of my first visit to Indonesia. I've never seen so many smiling faces. It's a beautiful and unique country, where everybody's very friendly, and has a smile for everyone. They could give a lesson to we Americans about how to be pleasant to each other. I'm now going home to prepare for my rematch with Joe Frazier...and I don't intend to be pleasant to him!'

EYEWITNESS – RUDI LUBBERS, 'Fighting Muhammad Ali was for me like being a hill climber suddenly tackling Mount Everest. I did not conquer the mountain but I had the satisfaction of trying to beat it. I will never forget the experience. It was so hot in the ring you could have friend an egg on the canvas. I did my best but I was up against The Greatest. I am very proud to have fought him.'

WHATEVER HAPPENED TO RUDI LUBBERS? Lubbers made the headlines for all the wrong reasons after retiring in 1981. He was sentenced to four years in prison for drug dealing in Portugal, and was declared bankrupt after his wife's funfair business went bust. Reduced to living in a caravan, he eventually became homeless. When his dire situation was reported friends rallied round and helped him get his life straight as he approached old age in relative comfort in Belgium. His ring record: Fights 36, wins 28 (13 stoppages), eight losses.

Joe Frazier (USA)

Venue: Madison Square Garden, NY
28 January 1974
Ali 212lb, Frazier 209lb
Ali WPTS12
(Ali purse: $1,715,000)

BILLED as Superfight II, this was considered the least exciting and compelling of the three contests between Ali and Frazier, yet it still came into the classic category. For three years Ali had been feeding off dreams of avenging his first defeat by Smokin' Joe, and there was the added incentive that the winner would be in line for a world title shot at the new king, George Foreman.

The build-up to the fight was laced with genuine bad temper to go with the ticket-selling spiel. During a live face-to-face interview from ABC Studios in New York City, Ali began winding up Frazier about their respective hospital stays after the first fight (according to Ali he spent ten minutes in the hospital, while Frazier stayed there for a month). It reached boiling point when Ali called Frazier ignorant, and during a furious exchange of insults they wrestled each other to the studio floor. Both were fined $5,000 by the New York State Athletic Commission for bringing boxing into disrepute, a contradiction if ever there was one. The worldwide publicity

157

was worth millions. Ali started the fight a 7/5 favourite and they battled in front of a wildly excited crowd of 20,748, generating a live gate of $1,052,688, and three times as much from a worldwide television and closed-circuit theatre audience. Right up to the first bell Ali kept up a monologue of menace, staring hard at Frazier and promising him 'a whupping'.

The pattern of the fight was established from the first round, Ali circling, jabbing and throwing combinations, and Frazier moving aggressively forward behind a high guard, bobbing and weaving in an attempt to get under Ali's longer reach and to land the lethal left hook that had dramatically floored Ali in the 15th round of their Garden epic three years earlier.

Frazier's devastating defeat by Foreman had not robbed him of any of his warrior-like confidence, and he continually marched forward while calling for Ali to 'stand and fight'. But while Joe was predictable and often ponderous in the first half of the fight, there were flashes of the old Louisville Lip as Ali danced and dazzled, seeming almost to enjoy himself while Joe ate his left jabs.

There was a controversial climax to the second round. Ali landed a straight right to Frazier's jaw with 20 seconds to go. He wobbled slightly as he retreated to the ropes with Ali in pursuit, but suddenly referee Tony Perez leapt between them and signalled for them to return to their corners.

'Somebody called "bell",' Perez explained later, 'so I stopped them fighting. Then the gong table yelled, "Tony, the round ain't over." Usually I hear the bell, but it had been defective before the fight. They had to call the electrician to fix it. I waved them to carry on fighting, but it was only a few seconds before the bell really did ring.'

Throughout the contest Frazier kept complaining to Perez that Ali was holding in the clinches. 'The only violation,' Perez said, 'is if you hold and hit at the same time. Ali was holding but he wasn't hitting.' Frazier's veteran trainer, Eddie Futch, continued the protests to Perez at every opportunity. The first four rounds were clearly Ali's, and the ever-aggressive Frazier was getting increasingly frustrated as the clever Kentuckian slipped most of his best shots. Smokin' Joe finally caught fire in rounds seven and eight as Ali took a breather, resting on the ropes and letting his angry and hungry opponent take the initiative with continual bombardments to the body.

Just as it looked as if Frazier was going to come from behind to snatch victory from the jaws of defeat, Muhammad got back up on his toes and danced out of range in the final rounds to clinch a unanimous decision. Judge Jack Gordon scored the fight 8-4, judge Tony Castellano 7-4-1, and referee Tony Perez had it 6-5-1.

ALI AFTER-FIGHT QUOTE, 'Who would have thought they were watching a 32-year-old? I had the legs and the energy of a much younger man and old Joe was puffin' and pantin' as I left him chasing my shadow. George Foreman will lose sleep after seeing that performance. He's just borrowing MY title.'

EYEWITNESS - JOE FRAZIER, 'No excuses, but the referee let Ali get away with murder. He was holding right through the fight, not allowing me to let go with my best punches. That's one-one. We still have business to settle.'

George Foreman (USA)

Venue: Kinshasa, Zaire
30 October 1974
Ali 217lb, Foreman 220lb
Ali WKO8
(Ali purse: $5m)

THIS was arguably the most remarkable and dramatic of all Ali's fights, and it brought into the English language two new phrases that survive to this day, 'The Rumble in the Jungle' and 'rope-a-dope'. The fight was staged in the unlikely setting of Kinshasa in Zaire, now the Democratic Republic of the Congo, and was noisily promoted by the larger-than-life Don King. He promised champion George Foreman and challenger Ali a purse of $5m each, money he did not have. So he turned to Zaire's flamboyant President, Mobutu Sese Seko, to sponsor the fight in return for putting his country on the world map.

And the rest of the world bought into King's imaginative idea in a big way. The fight was shown on closed-circuit television at 450 locations in the United States and Canada, and was televised live in 100 countries worldwide, with celebrity interviewer David Frost as the guest commentator. The world clock was not allowed to get in the way, and the boxers walked to the ring at 4am for a duel at dawn to accommodate the vast audiences in the United States.

The fight was originally arranged for 24 September, and both champion and challenger spent August getting acclimatised to the tropical African weather. But the showdown had to be put back five weeks when Foreman suffered a cut eye while sparring. This gave Ali longer to put psychological pressure on the champion, and he worked on winning himself an army of supporters among the adoring Congolese people, leading them in constant chants of 'Ali bomaye, Ali bomaye'. This translates as 'Ali, kill him'.

Foreman, with 'Ageless Archie' Moore in his corner as one of his seconds, let Ali do all the pre-fight talking, and just contented himself with saying, 'I'll do my talking with my fists. Ali will go the same way as Joe Frazier. He is playing with fire getting into the ring with me.'

Privately in his dressing room, Foreman led his team in a prayer in which he asked aloud, 'Dear Lord, while winning please do not let me go too far and kill Ali, despite the way he continually insults me.' George, 24 and at his physical peak, was genuinely convinced he was going to seriously hurt the aging challenger.

Ali was filling Foreman's ears with taunts and insults as referee Zack Clayton delivered his final instructions. If the fight was going to be decided by a war of words there could be only one winner, but ringside reporters were almost unanimous in their predictions that Foreman would carry too much ammunition for his chatterbox challenger.

Everybody expected Ali to get up on his toes and dance out of range of the champion's heavy artillery. Everybody was wrong. He continually interrupted his retreat to deliver right hand leads that first bemused and then confused Foreman, who kept on a one-track forward march without any lateral movement. While the swinging, clubbing champion clearly had the heavier punch, Ali's stinging blows were accompanied by screams from his new-found fans as if they were providing a percussion accompaniment.

We were introduced to Ali's controversial rope-a-dope tactics from the start of round two, when he leaned back on the ropes inviting Foreman to launch two-fisted attacks. It was a high-risk strategy, but Ali insisted he knew what he was doing as Angelo Dundee repeatedly yelled for him to 'get off the ropes'.

The fight now had a pattern that few had envisaged, George pounding away with both hands, while Ali lay as far back as the slack ropes would allow as he blocked, dodged and nullified the hail of leather coming his way. He kept up a continual mocking commentary, 'That all you got, George…if you can't do better than that you're in BIG trouble…I'll be coming to get you soon, George…You're just a big cissie.'

It was clear that Ali was waiting for Foreman to punch himself out, and his assaults became slower and slower with each passing round. He further tired the champion by leaning on him in the clinches, outwrestling him and using his old trick of pushing down on the neck so that George became disoriented and, finally, dispirited.

Though dominating most of the exchanges, Foreman was staggered by an Ali combination at the start of the fourth round and again near the end of the fifth, which was a rehearsal for what was to come in dramatic fashion in the final minute of the eighth.

Foreman was on the edge of exhaustion as he threw what were now pit-a-pat punches, with Ali lying in wait on the ropes. Suddenly a left hook counter brought George upright with a startled look on his face. Ali catapulted off the ropes and put everything into a straight right to the head. Foreman twisted round like a kid's spinning top and fell heavily on his back to the canvas. He was scrambling around like a drunk in a maze, and as he staggered up referee Clayton completed the ten-second count with George not knowing if he was in Timbuktu or Toledo.

It was an astonishing finish to an astonishing fight. Ten years after startling Sonny Liston and seven years after being stripped of the title, Ali had finally regained the world heavyweight championship.

ALI AFTER-FIGHT QUOTE, 'I told you all that I am The Greatest. Never ever doubt me again. I didn't dance tonight for the simple reason I wanted George to punch himself out. I got into his head and told him he was punching like a cissie. When a fighter gets in the ring, he has to adjust according to the conditions he faces. Dancin' all night, my legs would have got tired. And George was following me from too close, cutting off the ring. I've introduced a new tactic to boxing, and it's beautiful. I call it rope-a-dope, and poor George was the dope who fell for it. A couple of times he shook me bad, especially with the right hand. But I blocked and dodged most of what he threw, and each round his punches got slower and hurt less when they landed. I knew he had worn himself out.'

EYEWITNESS – GEORGE FOREMAN, 'A long time after the fight I could think of all sorts of excuses. The ring ropes were loose. The referee counted too fast. The cut hurt my training. I was drugged. But instead of being bitter I wish I'd just said the best man won, but I'd never lost before so I didn't know how to lose. He outfought me and outthought me. Muhammad has become my best friend in the world and I have nothing but respect for him. But that night in the jungle he sure got to me!'

WHATEVER HAPPENED TO GEORGE FOREMAN? He retired following a points loss to Jimmy Young in 1977, claiming to have had a religious epiphany. George became an ordained Christian minister. Ten years later he announced a comeback and, in November 1994, at age 45, he regained the world heavyweight title by knocking out Michael Moorer. He is the oldest heavyweight champion in history, and second oldest in any weight class after Bernard Hopkins. He retired for good in 1997 at the age of 48, with a final record of 76-5, including 68 knockouts. He concentrated on bringing up his 12 children, including five sons all called George. Then, as an entrepreneur, he struck gold, with his promotion of the George Foreman Grill, selling the naming rights for an incredible $138m. Old George had the last laugh.

Chuck Wepner (USA)

Venue: Richfield, Ohio
24 March 1975
Ali 223lb, Wepner 225lb
Ali WRSF15
(Ali purse: $1.6m)

ALI understandably wanted a comfortable first defence after his jungle warfare with Foreman but he got more of an argument than he expected from Chuck Wepner, the fighter who inspired the Rocky character portrayed at the cinema by Sylvester Stallone.

Wepner was an unheralded, brawling 36-year-old club fighter who had a full-time job as a liquor salesman. The 6ft 5in, 225lb ex-Marine from New Jersey had a chin carved out of rock, but his heavily scarred eyebrows cut easily and earned him the nickname the Bayonne Bleeder. To sell tickets Ali talked him up as the Great White Hope. Questioned on this by a disbelieving press, the champion repeated with tongue deeply in cheek, 'Yeah, he's the Great White Hope. Guess that's the only hope he's got.'

It was clear to all Aliphiles that the champion had not got himself into the best condition for the fight, and that he was obviously underestimating his challenger who was more noted for his stamina than any destructive punching power.

Ali toyed with Wepner through the first eight rounds, often teasing him with a pretence at being hurt and then letting fly with flurries of combinations that rocked him back on his heels. Wepner kept hitting and hoping and was having more success as the champion began to tire, mainly because of the surplus weight he was carrying.

The world held its breath in the ninth round when Wepner – walking through a mouthful of left jabs – landed with a right under the heart that caught Ali off balance. The champion fell backwards, his head hitting the bottom rope. He was later to claim that the challenger had trodden on his foot, but there was no doubt that it was a clean knockdown.

More embarrassed than hurt, Ali quickly got up but had to take a mandatory eight-count from referee Tony Perez. It was only the fourth time in his career that he had been on the canvas (following on from Sonny Banks, Henry Cooper and Joe Frazier…but the only time from a right-hand punch). The knockdown forced Ali to stop clowning and to take the fight seriously. He started to box with more purpose and dominated rounds ten through 15, picking his punches accurately as he rained long left leads and follow-through rights on to Wepner's flattened features.

The untidy contest was into its last minute when Ali decided to put on a show for his public and started to dazzle and daze Wepner with a vicious series of left hooks and right crosses. The exhausted challenger fell back against the ropes and slowly slumped to the canvas. He was struggling to get up but was so separated from his senses that he could not grab hold of the ropes to steady himself, and there were just 19 seconds of the final round left when the referee waved it all over.

ALI AFTER-FIGHT QUOTE, 'That was a stumble rather than a knockdown. He regretted doing it 'cos I decided I needed to punish him. I respected his bravery but he had no right to be in the same ring or even the same stadium as me. I'm gettin' old, but I remain The Greatest.'

EYEWITNESS - CHUCK WEPNER, 'I gave Ali the fright of his life. If I'd caught him just a little harder he'd have gone through the ropes and would not have been able to beat the count. Then I'd been champion of the world. He caught me some good shots at the end, but the ref could have let me see the fight out. I deserved to go the distance.'

WHATEVER HAPPENED TO CHUCK WEPNER? Wepner's gutsy performance against Ali inspired Sylvester Stallone to write the Oscar-winning film *Rocky*. It brought Chuck more fame than he'd ever had in the ring, but not a fortune and he was continually fighting to get a share of the box office takings.

He had nine more fights before retiring in 1978, with a 35-14-2 record. Seven years later he was arrested for possession of cocaine, and was given a ten-year sentence in March 1988. He served three years in Newark's Northern State Prison before being released. Wepner has been married to his third wife, Linda, since September 1994 and does public relations work for a pharmaceutical company and a packaging business in addition to giving motivational speeches.

'I've been clean now for more than 20 years,' says Wepner. 'I'm very lucky. I have my health, and though I was never a champ, I'm treated like one here in my own hometown of Bayonne.'

By his own count Chuck had 329 stitches around his eyes, and of his 14 losses eight were on stoppages caused by cuts.

In 2002 he was put on probation for his part in a scam selling forged Muhammad Ali autographs, and well into his 70s was selling his own genuine autograph to fans who admired his real Rocky adventure.

Ron Lyle (USA)

Venue: Las Vegas
16 May 1975
Ali 224lb, Lyle 219lb
Ali WRSF11
(Ali purse: $1m)

O NE of 19 children, Ron Lyle took a dramatic path to a world championship challenge against Muhammad Ali. While still in his teens he was convicted of second degree murder following a gang war shooting and he was sentenced to 15–25 years at the Colorado State Penitentiary. During his early days in prison, Lyle was knifed and underwent a seven-hour operation; twice pronounced dead on the operating table, he needed 36 pints of blood to keep him alive.

Boxing was Lyle's salvation and on his release at the age of 28 he quickly established himself as a powerhouse of a heavyweight, with a huge physique shaped and strengthened during hours of work in the prison gym. Impressive victories over Jimmy Ellis, Buster Mathis and Oscar Bonavena earned him his shot at Ali, and he grabbed it with both hands.

Ali tried his 'rope-a-dope' strategy, but Lyle would not play along and claimed the centre of the ring. The champion then switched to what he called his 'mirage' style of boxing, going to the middle of the ring, holding his hands up, palms together as if in supplication. He took Lyle's punches on the gloves and arms while peering out at his opponent. A sharp right uppercut through the gloves in the ninth round clearly troubled Ali and he abandoned the statuesque tactics and introduced some old-style floating and stinging moves while on the retreat.

It was developing into a lazy, uninspiring performance from the champion, and going into the 11th round most good judges at ringside had the challenger narrowly ahead on points.

Early in the 11th, Lyle shaped to throw a left jab but Ali beat him to it with his own left. It was the marker for a following right that landed perfectly on the point of the jaw and Lyle reeled backwards into the ropes.

Until this sudden explosion, Ali had looked almost disinterested, but now he was a man on a mission. He drove Lyle along the ropes, across the ring and into a neutral corner. The suddenly unhinged challenger was overpowered, unable to avoid the incoming hurricane of punches.

Ali turned to referee Ferd Hernandez and motioned for him to stop the fight. The referee refused, so Ali hit Lyle with a lightning left-right-left to the head, then stepped back again and waved to Hernandez. This time, wisely, the referee – under orders from a caring champion – stopped it. Lyle was out on his feet.

ALI AFTER-FIGHT QUOTE, 'I'm not in boxing to cause unnecessary pain and punishment. The referee's in there to protect the fighters. It was obvious I had Ron beat and that's why I encouraged the ref to step in and stop it. He ignored me at first, so I just had to make up his mind for him. That was tough on Ron, who had to take unnecessary punches. He gave me a hard time in there, but there was only ever gonna be one winner.'

EYEWITNESS – RON LYLE, 'All the judges had me ahead on their scorecards at the end, which proves I gave Ali a hell of a fight. I wasn't gonna fall for his rope-a-dope tricks. I saw what he did with Foreman, and I'd made up my mind if he was gonna lay on the ropes he could just stay there on his own. He caught me with a good shot in the 11th, and if I could just have got hold of him and hung on for a few moments I could have caused one of the upsets of the century. But, hey, that's boxing, that's life. Some you win, some you lose.'

WHATEVER HAPPENED TO RON LYLE? Lyle was back in the headlines in 1976 with a sensational war against George Foreman. Both were down twice before George won in the fifth round of a fight considered one of the most exciting and brutal in heavyweight history.

After Big George had regained the world title in 1994, Lyle made an unlikely comeback at the age of 54 with a second championship challenge and a return with George in mind. He won four contests in 1995 but the Foreman dream never materialised and Lyle retired for good having won 43 fights, lost seven and drawn one.

He worked as a security guard and a trainer in his later years, and was again accused of murder in 1978 after a former prison cell-mate was shot at Lyle's home. Ron claimed self defence and was acquitted. A biography of Lyle, *Off the Ropes: The Ron Lyle Story*, was published in 2010, a year before his death following stomach surgery on 26 November 2011. He was 70.

Joe Bugner (UK)

Venue: Kuala Lumpur, Malaysia
30 June 1975
Ali 224lb, Bugner 230lb
Ali WPTS15
(Ali purse: $2m)

TICKETS were selling so slowly for Ali's return fight with British heavyweight hope Joe Bugner in the steaming, humid capital of Malaysia that the champion announced, 'Anybody who wants to see the greatest heavyweight boxer in history in action had better be ringside, 'cos this is gonna be my last fight. I'm getting too old for this. I've got other things to do with my life.'

It was pure box office hokum aimed at getting bums on seats. Ali had already secretly agreed to a deciding showdown with Joe Frazier, who was at ringside swapping shouted insults with his old foe.

It was so scorching hot when Ali and Bugner stepped into the ring at 10am to satisfy the demands of the TV paymasters that you could have fried a breakfast on the canvas, and both boxers were understandably lethargic and fought in short bursts while they conserved energy. At times it was almost as if they were in a choreographed dance, with first one attacking from long range before retreating and allowing his opponent to take centre stage.

It was a battle of the jabs, with champion and challenger showing each other a healthy respect while grabbing every opportunity to take rests on the ropes. Every round had the same routine, Ali and then Bugner briefly getting on top before going into their shells to snatch lungfuls of air. The champion had the edge and was shading most of the rounds because he had the better variety of punches, often mixing in rat-a-tat combinations to go with his jabs.

There was a moment of hilarity out of the Ali school of unique humour in the 12th round. Bugner tried to rush the champion to the ropes. Ali turned him so cleverly that Joe was suddenly looking out into the crowd with his opponent behind him, and smacking Bugner on the backside as if he had been a naughty boy.

The three judges were unanimous in giving Ali a clear points decision (73-65, 73-67, 72-65), and Joe then took another hiding from the British media. They ridiculed his challenge, accusing him of not giving a totally committed performance, some of the criticism based on the fact that he swam 20 lengths in the hotel swimming pool within an hour of the fight and threw a champagne party for his friends.

Joe was fuming over the press coverage and made the point that he had got into the pool to help ease his bruises, and that the champagne had been laid on by the hotel not by him. He added, 'As so many of my friends and family had flown out to support me, the least I could do was give them an after-fight drink. The press chose to call it a party.'

ALI AFTER-FIGHT QUOTE, 'Joe has got a good chin and a good jab, and can be proud of his challenge considering the conditions. Only he and I and the referee know just how damn hot it was in there. It took all your energy just to get off the stool. Angelo was sweating so much I told him that he was going to finish up as a pool of water by the end of the fight. Changed my mind about retiring. Got some unfinished business with the gorilla, Joe Frazier and I'm gonna amaze yer .. we're gonna have a thrilla in Manila!'

EYEWITNESS - JOE BUGNER, 'It's so easy for those sitting outside the ring in the shade with their typewriters criticising, but it was 118 degrees under the ring lights. We did well to move let alone fight. Ali is as he keeps reminding us The Greatest, and I've now gone 27 rounds with him and held my own in both fights. I refuse to accept that I gave anything less than my best.'

WHATEVER HAPPENED TO JOE BUGNER? Joe regained the European heavyweight title with a one-round wipeout of Richard Dunn, and then searched for a new life, first of all in the United States and next in Australia, where he became naturalised and happily took on the nickname Aussie Joe. He got married for a second time to Marlene, a strong-minded woman who became his manager.

Joe retired from boxing in 1976, but over the next two decades made sporadic comebacks after a failed vineyard business venture left him broke. He beat fighters such as Greg Page, David Bey, Anders Eklund and James Tillis before retiring again after an eight-round stoppage by Frank Bruno in 1987. He made a final comeback during the 1990s, winning the Australian heavyweight title in 1995 and the WBF heavyweight championship in 1998 at the age of 48. He retired for the last time in 1999 with a final record of 69-13-1, including 43 wins inside the distance.

Joe Frazier (USA)

Venue: Manila
1 October 1975
Ali 224lb, Frazier 215lb
Ali WRTD 14
(Ali purse: $4.5m)

IT seemed improbable that Ali could get involved in a fight that surpassed the Rumble in the Jungle for drama and excitement, yet many consider this 'Thrilla in Manila' the most explosive, the most exhausting and most enthralling of all his contests. Many good judges rated it as the fight of the century, with both Ali and Frazier producing superhuman performances that took them to what the champion graphically described as 'the edge of death'.

Staged at the Araneta Coliseum in Quezon City, Metropolitan Manila, at 10.45am in scorching heat, the contest produced a bruising, brutal, breathtaking climax to the bitter three-fight rivalry between Ali and Frazier. In working at getting bums on seats, the champion went an insult too far when labelling the challenger as an 'Uncle Tom', the 'White Man's Champion' and an 'ugly dumb gorilla'. It infuriated Joe, who admitted his main motivation while training was a deep hatred for his mouth-on-legs opponent.

In just about every pre-fight interview, Ali chanted, 'It's gonna be a thrilla, and a chilla, and a killa, when I get the Gorilla in Manila.'

Much of the media attention leading up to the fight was centred on Ali's private life. It was widely reported that he was having a torrid affair with the beautiful Veronica Porche, and when his wife, Belinda, found out that Ali was introducing Veronica as 'Mrs Ali' she flew to the Philippines and confronted the champion in front of the world's media. This distraction convinced Frazier that Ali was ripe for the taking.

As the two sworn enemies came face to face in the centre of the ring for the referee's instructions, Ali continued his verbal assault and we could clearly hear him say, 'You don't have it, Joe, you don't have it! I'm going to put you away!'

Frazier made his customary slow start and was trailing at the end of the first two rounds after walking into a procession of hard left jabs and follow-through rights, two of which had him wobbling. But fears of his early demise proved unfounded as he started to duck and weave inside Ali's long punches and fire away two-fisted to the body.

Ali continued to shoot from the lip and he had the nerve to taunt Frazier with a nursery rhyme, 'Ah one ah two and ah three…Jack be nimble and Jack be quick, Jack jump over the candlestick. Is that all you can give, Joe? Come on, you ugly gorilla – hit me!' He then waved Frazier on, making a circular gesture with his right hand as an invitation for him to come forward into a mouthful of leather.

In round three, the champion began to fall back on his rope-a-dope tactics that had worked so well against Foreman. Frazier accepted the opportunity to take free punches and landed his first substantial body shots of the fight. In the last minute of the round the champion suddenly came catapulting off the ropes Zaire-style and landed a volley of hard punches that rocked Frazier back on his heels. This was all-out war.

By the fifth round, the bobbing, bouncing Frazier had found his timing and rhythm and started to pummel Ali with solid hooks from close range. A right hand visibly shook the champion, who feigned astonishment and said, 'You can't do that, Joe. You ain't got no right hand.' It would have made a great comedy show but for the fact that they were trying to knock off each other's head. The bombs were really flying.

Early in the sixth round, Joe was bang on target with his favourite left hook, and Ali fell back into the ropes. It was as thunderous a punch as knocked Ali down in the final round of their first fight. He somehow managed to keep his composure and tie Joe up as he tried to add to the pain. Another left hook had Ali in trouble, but he smothered, held and jabbed until his head cleared. Then back to the comedy script. 'They told me Joe Frazier was washed up,' he said. Joe now played the comedian rather than the straight man and responded, 'They lied.' All this in the middle of one of the fiercest world heavyweight title fights anybody had ever witnessed.

Ali was beginning to visibly tire in the sweltering conditions, and as he sought rest and respite on the ropes, cornerman Angelo Dundee kept pleading aloud, 'Get off the damn ropes!'

Just as it looked as if the champion might be ready to fold under Frazier's constant bombardment, Ali found extra energy in the eighth round and it was Joe who gave ground after a vicious toe-to-toe exchange. But Ali was on the edge of exhaustion as Frazier battled back and forced him to cover up on the ropes as the bell ended one of the most vicious rounds of this brutal battle.

At the end of another no-quarter-given ninth round, a visibly tired Ali told Dundee in the corner, 'Man, this is the closest I've ever been to dying.' Across the ring Frazier's face was swollen like a grotesque mask, the damage caused by an accumulation of scores of punches.

There was no way the two brave warriors could maintain this pace. Finally, in the tenth round, Frazier began to show signs of extreme fatigue and Ali somehow found new energy. He started to dance in his butterfly-floating style and he unleashed a series of long-range combinations that bounced off Joe's bruised head. The challenger's eyes were now so swollen he was fighting half blind and could not see where Ali's punches were coming from.

It was now a question of how much longer the boxers could stand up to the pace, the punishment and the searing heat. The ring temperature under the television lights and scorching sun was hitting a merciless 120°F.

It was the 13th round that decided the winner and the loser. Two desperate right hand leads from Ali landed on Frazier's mouth and sent his gum shield flying across the ring. Suddenly there was the rare sight of Frazier taking a backward step and it inspired Ali to unload a non-stop volley of punches that had Frazier out on his feet as the bell came to his rescue.

Bravely – foolishly, many would say – the blind and bleeding Frazier came out for the 14th round, and Ali stood off and picked his punches with little coming back in return. It was sickening to watch, and among those in the stadium who could take no more was the challenger's chief second Eddie Futch. He refused to let a protesting Frazier leave his corner for the 15th and final round.

'I want him, boss,' Joe said through swollen lips. Futch replied, 'It's all over. No one will forget what you did here today.' He then reluctantly signalled the challenger's surrender to referee Carlos Padilla.

As Ali became aware that Frazier was being forced to retire and he was still champion, he got up from his stool, raised an arm in victory, and then collapsed on to the canvas, totally exhausted.

Yes, as Ali said, it was close to dying.

Eddie Futch, one of the most respected and experienced cornermen of all time, was close to tears as he told the media, 'Joe would go to the line with one arm cut off if you asked him to. But I couldn't allow it.

'There was a possibility that he could have gone on to be very seriously hurt and I could not allow that. He gave his all and wanted to continue despite hardly being able to see. He took terrible punishment in the last 30 seconds of the 14th round when Ali was able to take deliberate aim and land every time. Not even the world heavyweight championship is worth risking the future health of a man like Joe Frazier.

'We were privileged to see two great warriors going beyond human endurance in as hard a fight as I've ever seen in a lifetime in this noble sport. There was no loser tonight. In my eyes, both men left the ring as winners. Joe will not concede that he was beaten. It was the toughest decision I ever had to make to ignore his wishes to fight on and pull him out of there. We will tell our grandkids that we were there for the fight of the century.'

ALI AFTER-FIGHT QUOTE, 'Joe Frazier, I'll tell the world right now, brings out the best in me. I'm gonna tell ya, that's one helluva man, and God bless him. We went close to dying in that ring. We gave everything and then more. Joe Frazier is the greatest fighter in the world, next to me. He has my total respect. I apologise for some of the things I said before the fight, but it's my business to help the promotion. Anybody who bad-mouths Joe Frazier will have me to answer to. He's the bravest of the brave. Only I could have beaten him in that ring today. It was like being in a torture chamber and in the heat of hell.'

EYEWITNESS - JOE FRAZIER, 'Man, I hit him with punches that'd bring down the walls of a city. I can't stand the man. There was no need for all those insults before the fight 'cos we were on a guaranteed purse. But I've gotta say he's got a giant heart and a strong chin. Some of my punches came from all the way back home. Why should I consider retiring? I'm still the man, I've still got it. It was the heat in there that beat me as much as anything. Ali was ready to go, but I just couldn't see to land the pay-off punch.'

WHATEVER HAPPENED TO JOE FRAZIER? Joe hung up his gloves in 1976 following a second defeat by George Foreman. He made a brief comeback in 1981 before retiring for good with a ring record of 37 fights, 32 wins (27 inside the distance), four defeats, one draw. Foreman and Ali were the only men ever to defeat him.

He opened a successful gymnasium, trained his son Marvis to a world title challenge, made records as lead singer with The Knockouts, and had reconciliation with his nemesis Muhammad Ali.

In the 1970s, Joe made millions of dollars in the ring but much of his fortune disappeared in a series of poorly managed business deals, particularly in real estate, and his daughter, Jackie – a lawyer – battled to get his rightful share of profits that did not come his way.

Joe died of liver cancer in 2011, aged 67. A desperately ill Ali made it to the funeral, and said, 'The world has lost a great champion. I will always remember Joe with respect and admiration. Take no notice of all those things I said about him. I was selling tickets, that's all. We had some great fights. Joe Frazier is a legend.'

Jean-Pierre Coopman
(Belgium)

Venue: San Juan, Puerto Rico
24 March 1975
Ali 226lb, Coopman 206lb
Ali WKO5
(Ali purse: $1m)

THERE was a sensible school of thought that Ali should have retired after his war with Frazier, but he was not in the mood to get off the mountain. His roadshow rolled on to San Juan, Puerto Rico, where he put his title on the line against Jean-Pierre Coopman, who did not have the credentials to be sharing the same ring as The Greatest. A stonemason admired for his strength rather than his skill, the thick-set Belgian heavyweight had lost three of his 27 previous fights and had never been in the ring with anybody near the class and quality of Ali.

The publicity department went into overdrive and dreamt up the nickname for Coopman of the Lion of Flanders. This came as something of a surprise to the mild-mannered Belgian, who had achieved little in the ring to justify such a warrior-like moniker. He was outweighed by 20lb, stood three inches shorter and was outreached by five inches. It was, in all honesty, a complete mismatch, yet such was the pulling power of the champion that 10,000 spectators crammed into the Coliseum and another 11,500 paying customers watched on closed circuit in a stadium next door.

The fight was little more than a public sparring session for Ali, and he clowned so much that his brother, Rachman, kept pleading in an anxious voice from the champion's corner for him to 'be tough'. Ali eventually looked down at him and ordered between showboating, 'Shut up!' He was doing all his talking to the corner because Coopman could not speak a word of English, so it would have been a waste of words trying his usual psychological patter.

Ali, looking flabby and shaking off the effects of a heavy cold, struggled to take the fight seriously when it was so obvious that he was fighting an opponent out of his depth. He taunted and tantalised the outclassed Belgian, who threw hopeful punches that the champion allowed to whistle inches away from his jaw.

At the end of the fourth round his manager, Herbert Muhammad, sent a 'stop fooling around' message to the corner, and Ali came out for the fifth session with a rapid finish on his agenda. For the first time he brought the heavy artillery into play, and he put the brave, outgunned Coopman out of his misery with a classic right uppercut late in the fifth. The punch came at the climax of a blindingly fast six-punch combination and the Belgian sunk slowly to the canvas, in a mixed state of confusion and concussion. The Lion of Flanders had gone out like a lamb.

A concerned Ali helped guide him back to his corner as he rose after the ten-second count on legs that were betraying him. Throughout his career, Ali rarely threw a more devastating uppercut.

ALI AFTER-FIGHT QUOTE, 'I felt bad when the fight was over. As Coopman fell I was sorry for him. He's a good fellow. He's got a wife. She was cryin'. His mother was cryin'. I hate to fight, but I got to have money, got to have fame so people pay to come to see me, got things need doin'. Those who say I should retire don't realise I have important things still to do for charity. I'm buildin' a school, and I'm buildin' a hospital. I need money. Not for me, but for good causes. I got a million for this fight, but look what's left. Taxes cut it to $600,000 here, and my expenses and taxes at home knock it down to $350,000. Then out comes my manager's end. I can't go on forever, but I'm gonna raise some hell and a lot of money while I can.'

EYEWITNESS - JEAN-PIERRE COOPMAN, 'I was not unconscious, but I could not get up. It felt like a heavy bag had me pinned down. I did as well as I could against a master boxer. It's an experience I'll never forget, and I'd like to thank Ali for giving me a shot at the championship. I just wish I could have landed my best punches, but he was just never there to be hit. Yes, he really is The Greatest.'

WHATEVER HAPPENED TO JEAN-PIERRE COOPMAN? He lost 12 of 26 fights after his defeat by Ali, and briefly held the European heavyweight title. Coopman then returned to his first love as a stonemason and sculptor and worked on reparations at medieval Belgian churches. He was also in demand as a portrait painter of famous boxers, with his study of Muhammad Ali taking prime place in his exhibitions. It was the only time he had Ali on the canvas. Ring record: 54 fights, 36 wins (23 inside the distance), 16 defeats, two draws.

Jimmy Young (USA)

**Venue: Landover, Maryland
30 April 1976
Ali 230lb, Young 209lb
Ali WPTS15
(Ali purse: $1.6m)**

THE next stop on Ali's 'take the money and run' agenda was scheduled to be Costa Rica, but after a dispute over a cash guarantee promoter Don King switched the fight to the equally unlikely venue of Landover in Maryland. Waiting in the opposite corner was Philadelphian prospect Jimmy Young, who was seven years younger than Ali and was expected to at least give the champion a workout. He had outpointed world-ranked Ron Lyle and held Earnie Shavers to a draw in a return fight after being blasted out in round one of their first encounter.

It was obvious at the weigh-in that Ali had not got himself in his best shape for this sixth defence since winning the title back from George Foreman. He scaled 230lb, his heaviest to date, and there was plenty of spare flesh on show as he tried to dance and jab against an opponent 21lb lighter and at his physical peak.

Young, a 15/1 underdog, followed a strategy of trying to frustrate Ali, ducking his head low whenever the champion attacked, and retreating after throwing sneak counter punches.

It was not pretty to watch, but it was effective and Ali was clearly unsettled and unable to find any of his usual rhythm.

When they got to close range, Young would spoil and neutralise Ali's usual supremacy by being passive and just concentrating on not getting hit. It was unusual to see Ali not dictating the tactics, and referee Tom Kelly was kept busy by issuing warnings for both fighters holding, and he got exasperated with the challenger for continually ducking below his opponent's waist.

Whenever the slipping and sliding Young was backed up against the ropes, he would lean back with his head outside the ring in his own peculiar version of rope-a-dope. The referee eventually stopped him from using this nullifying tactic by counting in the 12th round until he pulled his head back in from beneath the top rope and resumed a conventional fighting stance.

It was without question the untidiest and messiest of all Ali's fights, and Young's carefully plotted negative methods were the main reason it was such a poor spectacle. But from the challenger's perspective he had found a way of robbing Ali of his famous rhythm, and while not satisfying to watch it gave him almost equality in the dull, long-range exchanges.

Carrying so much extra weight, Ali visibly tired and Young came out of his defensive shell and started to score heavily in the closing stages. The challenger's corner celebrated as if they had won the championship at the final bell and there was widespread booing in the crowd when a unanimous decision was awarded to Ali.

Referee Kelly scored it 72-65; judges Larry Barrett and Terry Moore had it 70-68 and 71-64, respectively. Ed Schuyler Jnr, renowned ringside reporter with Associated Press, scored the fight 69-66 for Young.

ALI AFTER-FIGHT QUOTE, 'I didn't train like I should have done. I underestimated him. The experts dismissed him as a 15/1 underdog but he didn't fight like one. I weigh 230lb, just what I weigh when I'm in terrible shape. I've been eating too much pie, too much ice cream. I'm 34, an old man, and I'm telling you what

I did was a miracle, going 15 rounds and beating that young man. It was close but there's no doubting that I won it. When I retire he is the man who can take over as champion.'

EYEWITNESS – JIMMY YOUNG, 'I gave it my all and feel as if I've been robbed. He had me dazed a couple of times but never had me in any real trouble, and there were many times when I hurt him and had him holding on. I don't know what fight the judges were watching. I am thankful to Ali for giving me a shot at the championship, now I'd like him to give me a rematch. I've earned it.'

WHATEVER HAPPENED TO JIMMY YOUNG? Young went on to beat George Foreman on points in a 12-round war in 1977, then it was mostly downhill from there as he lost to Ken Norton, twice to Ossie Ocasio, and became a stepping stone for the likes of Gerry Cooney, Greg Page, Tony Tucker, and Tony Tubbs. He made a couple of comebacks before hanging up his gloves in 1986 with a record of 56 fights, 34 wins, 19 losses, two draws and one no contest.

Jimmy ran into financial, drug and legal problems, and his defence attorney revealed during a court case that he was suffering from 'traumatic brain damage'. Jimmy died following a heart attack in 2005. He was 56.

Richard Dunn (UK)

**Venue: Olympiahalle, Munich
24 May 1976
Ali 220lb, Dunn 206lb
Ali WRSF5
(Ali purse: $1.6m)**

IN April 1976, Yorkshireman Richard Dunn fought German champion Bernd August in London for the European title vacated by Joe Bugner, with the added prize that the winner would meet Muhammad Ali for the world crown. The Ali fight had already been confirmed for Munich with the undefeated August expected to be the opponent. There was no way, so the Germans thought, that he could lose to Dunn, whose career had largely followed the Baron de Coubertin principle of the importance of taking part rather than winning.

Dunn threw a spanner – no, a pickaxe – in the works with a swinging right hand that separated the shambling alp August from his senses, the referee having to rescue him as he stumbled around the ring in the third round. Poor old August was one of life's losers – just a few years later he was killed in Australia when his motorbike collided with a kangaroo.

It was the $4m punch from Dunn. That is how much it cost the German promoters when they stubbornly and stupidly

185

went ahead and put on Ali's title defence in a midnight fight in Munich.

I try to hide it on my CV that I worked on this fight as a publicist, as it was the biggest money-loser of any championship contest staged in Europe. The German public were just not interested in watching a virtually unknown Brit, even though the legend that was Ali provided the opposition.

The stadium would have been less than half full if Ali had not gone to American military bases giving away tickets by the fistful.

My brief from my fee-payers ViewSport – masterminded by entrepreneur Jarvis Astaire – was to drum up business for the cinemas screening the fight in Britain (note on CV: ViewSport made a profit).

Ali flew into Munich with an entourage of 54 – family, friends, sparring partners, souvenir-sellers, hangers-on, all of them running up the sort of promotion-paid expenses that make our MPs seem like amateurs. Ali's chief representative was a charismatic charmer called Butch Lewis, who was like a sawn-off version of Ali, full of chat and always wearing a smart tie but no shirt. Damon Runyan would have been in his element with this cast of characters.

Now enter the story one of the more astonishing people to cross my path, a hypnotist called Romark. He had been on the sports pages the previous year when Crystal Palace manager Malcolm Allison invited him to put the players under his spell.

It all ended acrimoniously, with Romark claiming Allison had not paid him the promised fee for his hypnotic deeds and he put a curse on Palace. Some believe the curse of Romark is still working at Selhurst Park to this day.

This was the same Romark who once boasted that he could drive through London blindfolded. He actually managed 30 yards before crashing into the back of a parked vehicle that just happened to be a police car.

The Daily Mirror had led the way on the Romark–Palace saga and I suggested to their boxing correspondent Ron Wills that it would be a good idea for them to pay for Romark to come to Munich to hypnotise Richard Dunn. What nobody had told me was that earlier in the year Romark suffered a stroke that had left his face contorted, with one eye lower than the other. Not a pretty sight.

He had been brought over to Munich for the express purpose of trying to convince Dunn he could cause the biggest upset in boxing history, but Romark had more grandiose ideas. Without a word to anybody, he decided he could put Ali under his influence.

As we walked through a corridor of the Hilton on the day of the weigh-in, Romark and I just happened to find Ali walking towards us with trainer Angelo Dundee. As I started to exchange pleasantries, Romark suddenly confronted him and – seven inches shorter than the champ – said with as wide a stare as he could muster, 'You are doomed to defeat tonight. D-o-o-m-e-d.'

Ali fell to his knees laughing uncontrollably, while Dundee asked, 'Who is this nutter?'

'He's our secret weapon,' I said, trying hard to keep a straight face – something beyond the powers of the stricken Romark.

Ali and Dundee continued to the weigh-in, where his huge entourage joined him. So many people climbed on to the stage that it collapsed under their combined weight, luckily without any serious injury. Romark meaningfully touched the side of his nose to suggest that he had something to do with it.

Later that afternoon, he tucked Richard Dunn up in bed and told him a fairy story as he sent the challenger to sleep. ('I pretended I had drifted off,' Richard confided later. 'The bloke was completely barmy. He kept telling me I had fists of iron.')

When the Dunn team got to the stadium, they were annoyed to find an American TV crew in their dressing room. Manager George Biddles ordered them out and while the cameraman continued to focus on Richard, his trainer and father-in-law Jimmy Devanney turned off the dressing-room lights.

This backfired because Richard was now sitting in the darkened dressing-room while high on a wall facing him a TV monitor was showing live pictures of Muhammad Ali telling the viewers just what he intended to do to his challenger.

Ali had got himself in shape for the fight, shedding ten pounds after his undistinguished performance against Jimmy Young just 24 days earlier. All the time he was in Germany, I noticed that Ali lived, ate and trained as if he was on American time and he didn't alter his watch or his sleeping habits. The media thought he was not training properly, not realising that he was going to the gymnasium in the middle of the night for his sparring sessions.

Dunn put up a gallant, beyond-the-call-of-duty performance before being stopped in five rounds. He forced Ali back in the opening two rounds with a non-stop two-fisted attack and we wondered if his southpaw stance was going to prove too much of a puzzle for the champion. But Ali started to find the range and had the brave Brit down for three counts in the fourth.

As he stood waiting for the bell to signal the start of the fifth round, Ali was miming across the ring to Dunn, showing him where he intended to drop him.

He then proceeded to provide action to go with his threat and the referee came to the rescue after Dunn had been floored twice by heavy combination punches. Little did we know that these would be the last knockdowns of his career recorded by Ali.

I climbed into the ring at the end of the fight to collect the champion's gloves as Angelo Dundee pulled them off. They were to be signed for charity.

Later that night I took them to Ali's bedroom in the Hilton, and sat on his bed – his lady of the time between the covers – as the champion autographed the gloves and a book for me. Inside the right glove, written before the fight, were the words: Ali wins. Inside the left glove, the result: wko5.

It was 3am when I went down to the foyer just as Richard Dunn arrived after a medical check-up. He was met by a posse of hard-bitten British pressmen, who melted and gave him a round of thunderous applause. Hypnotist Romark, tears streaming down his contorted face, pushed his way through the crowd of reporters and cuddled an embarrassed Dunn. 'I let you down, Richard,' he sobbed. 'I made your fists turn into iron – but I forgot about your chin.'

There was no happy ending for Romark, real name Ronald Markham. He later had another stroke and died after being imprisoned for embezzling his mother.

ALI AFTER-FIGHT QUOTE, 'Dunn can be proud of his performance. He gave me some anxious moments in the early rounds, and hit me with some good shots. But I was just bidin' my time, and knew I would take him out once I got my timing right. I'm sorry there were not more in the stadium to see the fight, but I guess it would have made more sense to have fought in London. Why would the Germans want to come out at that time of night to see an American beating up a Brit? I guess if August had been my opponent it would have been a sell-out, but Dunn earned the right to the fight and represented himself and his country well.'

EYEWITNESS – RICHARD DUNN, 'It was the greatest night and experience of my life. I landed some really big punches to Ali's head, but he has a chin of steel. Romark got nowhere near hypnotising me. I kidded him he had sent me to sleep just so he would leave me alone. He was as mad as a March hare. I lost but I don't think I let anybody down. Ali really is The Greatest, and I got to rock him a couple of times. If I'd fought him at home, I'd have done even better.'

WHATEVER HAPPENED TO RICHARD DUNN? Dunn lost his next fight to Joe Bugner, surrendering his British, European and Commonwealth titles in a stunning first-round knockout defeat. He retired after one more contest, a fifth-round stoppage by big-hitting Kallie Knoetze in the Ellis Park Tennis Stadium in Johannesburg.

He remains a huge hero in his hometown of Bradford, where a sports centre is named after him. A hotel business he set up with his loyal wife, Jan, failed, and Richard is now living in Scarborough after surviving a 40-foot fall while working on a North Sea oil rig. He is a likeable man with a huge heart, but like so many others, he was not in Ali's class. Ring record: 45 fights, won 33 (16 inside the distance), lost 12 (11 stoppages).

Ken Norton (USA)

Venue: Yankee Stadium, New York
28 September 1976
Ali 221lb, Norton 217lb
Ali WPTS15
(Ali purse: $6m)

THIS was the last fight staged at the original Yankee Stadium, and took place on what was considered one of the wildest nights in the history of the famous old ballpark. There was a police strike and unsupervised, intoxicated fans brawled inside and outside the stadium. Promoter Bob Arum blamed what he described as 'an unruly mob' for the fact that only 19,000 of the 30,000 who had bought tickets got to their seats.

Ali, an 8/5 betting favourite, was contemptuous of Norton before this third and deciding fight between the two bitter rivals. Norton had broken Ali's jaw when outpointing him in their first meeting, and Muhammad had evened the score with a narrow points victory. 'I'll knock the sucker out inside five rounds this time,' the champion promised, but failed to put action to go with his words against the man he was later to describe as 'my most difficult opponent'.

Those who cared about Ali and his health were concerned that he insisted on continuing his career. His long-time personal physician and close confidant Dr Ferdie Pacheco told me before the showdown with Norton, 'I've recommended that Ali retire. I'm worried about liver and kidney damage with all those body blows he takes, but the great man will not listen to me. I'm going to quit his camp to try to bring him to his senses.'

Ali was deaf to the advice and warnings, and allowed Norton free hits to his body as he lay on the ropes conserving energy in a fight fought at a pedestrian pace and without the skill and passion of their two previous battles.

The champion abandoned his early tactics of trying to force Norton back and resorted to laying on the ropes in the middle rounds, absorbing the punishment from two-fisted body attacks and catching Norton with sudden counter punches. It was not until the 11th round that Ali produced his trademark dancing and dominating from long range.

At one stage Norton, not usually a showman, started to imitate Ali, shouting insults at the champion and clown-boxing. But he quickly realised it did not suit him and he went back to his spoiling, crab-like style that frustrated Ali through much of their three fights.

It developed into a tough, bruising battle for both boxers, and going into the final round it was difficult to pick between them. Referee Arthur Mercante and the two judges scored the last session for Ali to give him a hugely disputed points victory, a verdict that brought a storm of booing from a large section of the rowdy crowd.

Norton was in tears as he returned to his cramped dressing-room, usually used by the baseball umpires. He felt as if he'd been robbed, and there were no umpires to signal a strikeout.

ALI AFTER-FIGHT QUOTE, 'I did just enough to win. Only just but I remain champion of the world. Norton is always a tough opponent, but I've proved I'm his master. Now I must seriously consider retiring. I'm beginning to feel very old. I've got movies to make and so many things to do. The end is near. Catch me while you can. You'll never see another boxer in my class.'

EYEWITNESS - KEN NORTON, 'I won at least nine or ten rounds. I was robbed. You know I won it, I know I won it, even Ali knows I won it. I outfought him completely. Look at me, I'm not even breathing heavy. I worked so hard in the gym for this that I knew I was good and ready to take him. Ali was exhausted in there, and took a beating. Only time he hurt me was when he thumbed me in the eye. I know in my heart and soul that I am the winner and should be hailed as the world champion.'

WHATEVER HAPPENED TO KEN NORTON? He was declared WBC heavyweight champion in 1978 without throwing a punch. He was awarded the championship on the strength of a points victory months earlier over Jimmy Young and because of the failure of Leon Spinks to defend the title against him. He lost the crown in his first defence in a brutal battle with Larry Holmes. Ken had five more fights, and one-round stoppages by first Earnie Shavers and then Gerry Cooney convinced him he should hang up his gloves at the age of 37. He became a ringside TV summariser and an actor who landed several Hollywood roles. His son, Ken Jnr, was an outstanding NFL football linebacker. Ring record: 50 fights, 42 wins (33 inside the distance), seven defeats, one draw.

In 1986, a car accident almost killed him. He suffered multiple injuries, including a fractured skull and a brain injury that left him with slurred speech. This great athlete finally died following a series of strokes in 2013. He was 70.

Alfredo Evangelista (Uruguay)

Venue: Landover, Maryland
16 May 1977
Ali 221lb, Evangelista 209lb
Ali WPTS15
(Ali purse: $2.75m)

IF there were a vote for the most boring and pointless of Muhammad Ali's 61 fights this meaningless match against South American globetrotter Alfredo Evangelista would win by a yawning gap. Alfredo's main claim to fame is that he was the first Uruguayan to challenge for the world heavyweight title, but he had only one of his 78 fights in his homeland and was better known on the European circuit as a Spanish-based fighter. He challenged Ali in only his 17th contest, and at 22 was 13 years younger than the now veteran champion.

The publicists hurt their brains trying to give Evangelista a compelling image, and came up with the nickname the Lynx of Montevideo, but he fought more like a sphinx with little mobility or menace. He had been outpointed by the undistinguished Italian journeyman Lorenzo Zanon in his previous fight, but as it was in far-off Bilbao the promoters turned a blind eye to the defeat.

Ali treated the title defence as a glorified public sparring session and gave an exhibition of all his float-like-a-butterfly movement but none of the sting of the bee. He danced on his toes for ten of the 15 tedious rounds, and when he took breathers in the other five by laying on the ropes Evangelista had neither the power nor the skill to take advantage.

It reached the point where the champion was deliberately hanging his chin out for Alfredo to have a free hit, but the cautious Uruguayan, who had just come to survive, thought it was a trick and refused to accept the invitation.

There were a lot of jeers and boos from the 12,000 crowd, who were unimpressed by Ali's performance that by his sky-high standards lacked sparkle and energy. He had already committed himself to a much tougher defence against the fearsome Earnie Shavers, and he kept Evangelista at a distance to avoid the risk of cuts.

The judges were agreed on it being a walkover win for Ali. Ray Klingmeyer and Terry Moore both scored it 72-64, and referee Harry Oecchin made it 71-65 to the champion. Evangelista's consolation was that he earned a career-best purse of $85,000, which was ten times his previous highest payday.

For one of the few times in his career, Ali left the ring to boos ringing in his ears. Many of the spectators felt they had been cheated, paying for what turned out to be a training session. Evangelista and his cornermen celebrated at the final bell as if they had won the title. His one aim had been to remain on his feet for the 15 rounds.

ALI AFTER-FIGHT QUOTE, 'You saw a miracle tonight. I'm 35 years old and I danced 15 rounds. A middleweight couldn't dance 15 rounds. A welterweight couldn't either. Yet I did it against a young man who was not the bum you press reporters made out. Give him credit. He fought a good fight, but could not get near me. It was as if the years had fallen off me as I danced like a butterfly and gave the spectators the Ali shuffle. I am still the greatest dancing heavyweight the world has ever seen. Yes, it's a miracle.'

ALFREDO EVANGELISTA

EYEWITNESS - FERDIE PACHECO, 'Sadly, this fight proves I am right in saying Ali needs to quit before he gets seriously hurt. In fact the damage has already been done, judging by the way he is beginning to slur his words and all those body shots he takes can only damage his liver and kidneys. The old Ali would have got Evangelista out of there in five rounds, tops. He was just an empty shell of the great fighter we knew and loved. I still love the guy and just wish he would retire and enjoy his fame.'

WHATEVER HAPPENED TO ALFREDO EVANGELISTA? The tough-as-teak Uruguayan fought on until 1988, when the European Boxing Union revoked his licence following a two-round brawl in Madrid with novice Brooklyn heavyweight Arthur Wright. Alfredo won the majority of his fights but would always come unstuck when put in with top fighters like Larry Holmes (lko7, WBC title), Leon Spinks (lko5) and Greg Page (lko2).

Evangelista later had several run-ins with the law, eventually resulting in his imprisonment for drugs-related offences. He got his life back on track and spent his time between his adopted homeland of Spain and his birthplace of Montevideo, where he was reunited with a brother he had not seen for 30 years. Ring record: 78 fights, 61 wins (41 inside the distance), 13 defeats, four draws.

Earnie Shavers (USA)

**Venue: Madison Square Garden, NY
29 September 1977
Ali 225lb, Shavers 211lb
Ali WPTS15
(Ali purse: $3m)**

EARNIE SHAVERS was the most feared puncher in the heavyweight division, and there were many good judges who thought he could take out the fading Ali. He had wrecked 52 of his first 60 opponents with his hurricane hitting and all his opponents treated him with guarded respect – apart, of course, from the unique Ali.

Earnie had a shaved head, and the Louisville Lip nicknamed him The Acorn. As referee Johnny LoBianco was giving his pre-fight instructions in the middle of the ring, Ali leaned forward and kept polishing Earnie's gleaming bald head with the palm of his glove. It was comical, it was contemptuous and it gave Ali a huge psychological advantage before a punch had been thrown.

Crafty Angelo Dundee got to hear that NBC were going to flash the official scoring on the screen after every round. He stationed a friend in the champion's dressing room to watch the TV in there and relay the scores after each round. Going into the last third of the fight, Dundee knew the only way Shavers could beat his man was by a knockout. Ali produced what was now his common mix of being a ringmaster and a layabout, one minute up on his toes taunting and tantalising the aggressive, stalking Shavers with swift slippin' and slidin' movement and then, when needing to catch his breath, laying on the ropes and daring the challenger to risk getting rope-a-doped, Foreman-style.

Shavers was standing square and Ali could not miss him with his incessant and irritating left jab that piled up the points in the middle rounds. It was far from one-sided, but Ali always seemed to have a slight edge and it was noticeable that it was the power punching Shavers who was usually first to break off exchanges when they stood toe to toe swapping huge blows. Even when the action was at its most explosive Ali found time to clown, rubbing Earnie's head and saying aloud to his opponent, 'Acorns fall in September!'

Everybody wondered how Ali would react if Shavers caught him flush with his mighty right hand. It was detonated in the second round, but Ali fooled his opponent into thinking he was faking as he sagged against the ropes. Earnie was forced to wait until the 15th and final round before he got home again with his pet punch. Ali wobbled and stumbled after taking a punch that would have knocked most boxers cold. He showed amazing powers of recovery and immediately came back with a furious fusillade of punches that had Shavers hanging on to save himself from a knockdown.

It was a unanimous points win for the champion, judges Eva Shain and Tony Castellano scoring it nine rounds to six for Ali, while referee LoBianco called it for Ali by eight rounds to six, with one even. He had nullified the power of one of the hardest punchers in heavyweight history.

ALI AFTER-FIGHT QUOTE, 'So many people said Earnie would break me up with his big punches. This old man, many of you said, would not be able to take the sort of blows that have left his opponents wrecked. But he did not worry me more than a couple of times. One of his punches shook up my kinfolk in Africa, but there's nobody with a stronger chin than mine. I took the best he could give and came back stronger than him, and I had him in big trouble several times. The Acorn didn't quite fall in September, but he got rocked and was mighty glad to hear the final bell.'

EYEWITNESS - EARNIE SHAVERS, 'You just can't win against Ali. The judges only see him. That was a robbery. No way did he beat me. There were only a couple of times when he had me hurt, while I shook him up in most of the rounds. I did not get to hit him with my best punches, but still had him rocking. The referee let him get away with all his holding tricks. I was conserving my energy in there for the second half of the fight, but I just couldn't land the one punch that would have settled it. I like and admire Ali, but tonight I feel I've been robbed.'

WHATEVER HAPPENED TO EARNIE SHAVERS? Earnie, beaten in 11 rounds by Larry Holmes in a second title challenge, retired in 1983 because of retinal problems. He became an ordained Christian minister and moved to Phoenix, and later to England as a pastor. He combined his preaching with working as head of security for a Liverpool nightclub. After returning to the USA he was a 'meeter and greeter' in Las Vegas, and became a close friend of his old rival Ali. His ring record: 89 fights, 74 wins (68 by ko, and 23 inside the first round), 14 defeats, one draw.

Leon Spinks (USA)

**Venue: Hilton Hotel, Las Vegas
15 February 1978
Ali 224lb, Spinks 197lb
Ali LPTS15
(Ali purse: $3.5m)**

IN a monumental case of underestimating an opponent, Muhammad Ali lost his precious world crown to a virtual newcomer to the professional ranks in Leon 'Neon' Spinks. This was only the eighth professional fight for Spinks, making him world heavyweight champion in the shortest time in history from debut to title.

A split points victory to Spinks was one of the most stunning and surprising results ever. Even though Leon and his brother Michael had enjoyed double golden glory in the 1976 Montreal Olympics there were few boxing followers who gave him a chance against the legend that was Ali. He had not even managed to win all his seven fights, being held to a draw by Scott LaDoux, who was not a household name in his own household.

Here's a startling stat that underlines just how dominating Ali had been: Spinks was the only fighter ever to take the title from Ali in the ring. His other defeats were either as challenger or in non-title contests.

Aging before our eyes, Ali was clearly out of shape as he struggled to keep pace with the 12-years-younger Spinks, who had got himself to the peak of fitness and hounded and pounded the creaking champion for long periods of a fight fought at a frantic pace. Encouraged from the corner by his brother Michael, Leon never lost his concentration or composure. Even when Ali was digging deep to find extra energy and stamina, Spinks stuck to his fight strategy and kept an accurate left hand working that would have caught the eyes of the judges.

It was one of the few occasions when Ali finished a fight with a bruised and puffy face, evidence that many of the looping, long-range shots from Spinks had found their target. The champion had tried tiring out Spinks by drawing him into his rope-a-dope web, but Leon was well trained to avoid the trap, and Ali was forced to get on his dancing toes to try to sap his young opponent's energy.

Only Ali's incredible willpower kept him in the fight, and it was fairly even until the last three rounds when the younger man's superior fitness and drive came into play. As they answered the bell for the 15th and final round Ali sensed that he was in danger of losing and came out all guns blazing. But every time he looked on the point of knocking out Spinks, the ex-Marine would come back with a flurry of punches to steal the points. Ali had been here before, relying on the judges to come down in his favour, and he just hoped he had come up with the miracle recovery.

The 5,298 spectators held their breath when it was announced as a split decision. Judge Art Lucie scored it 143-142 for Ali. Judge Lou Tabat went 145-140 for Spinks.

Few in the audience heard the deciding score because they erupted at the words 'new heavyweight champion of the world'. For the record, judge Harold Buck scored it 144-141 for Spinks.

Suddenly, the Spinks gap-toothed grin – missing his two front teeth from boyhood – became a worldwide image. This was the man who had dethroned The Greatest.

ALI AFTER-FIGHT QUOTE, 'I let him rob my house while I was out to lunch. I seriously underestimated him, but he's only borrowing the title. I know my time is near when I have to retire, but I'm good for a fight or two more. I want to be the first man ever in the whole history of boxing to win the world heavyweight championship three times. That's my new motivation. I've been a true fighting champion. Never ducked nobody. I've given everybody a shot. Now I hope I'm given the chance to regain MY title. It's not the end of the world. It's a new beginning.'

EYEWITNESS - LEON SPINKS, 'I worked hard for this. Won it in the gymnasium and on the road. My brother Michael deserves a lot of the credit 'cos he's trained alongside me, inspiring and encouraging me. I knew if I could get myself fit enough I could outlast Ali. He can't dance forever, and I was not gonna fall for his rope-a-dope tricks. We knew what we had to do and we did it, and I thank God for my victory. I'm ready to give him a shot at the title. He was good enough to give me the chance and he deserves a return. I didn't think anything could get better than winning an Olympic gold medal. But it just got a lot better! I'm the latest, but Ali's still The Greatest.'

Leon Spinks (USA)

Venue: New Orleans
15 September 1978
Ali 221lb, Spinks 201lb
Ali WPTS15
(Ali purse: $3.5m)

ALI could always see the bigger picture. While all his followers were mourning his defeat by Leon Spinks, he had the vision and the imagination to recognise this was an opportunity to add to his legend. No fighter in history had won the world heavyweight boxing championship three times. But then, there had never been another fighter like Muhammad Ali. With the history-making scenario in mind, there was no way he was going to allow Spinks to become the first opponent ever to beat him twice.

To add to his confidence, Ali fed on the stories coming from the Spinks camp that Neon Leon was enjoying the nightlife and bright lights and had not stopped partying since winning the title. Ali vowed that the party would soon be over.

A 63,350 crowd packed into Louisiana Superdome to witness what the majority were desperately hoping would be 'the third coming'. It was not just a fight, it was a happening and the ringside was littered with celebrities like Jackie Onassis and President Carter's mother, film stars John Travolta and Kris Kristofferson, and a posse of politicians hoping some of Ali's popularity would rub off on them.

They saw Ali turning the clock back. He had punished himself in training to get into his best shape for several years, and he boxed with all his old skill and impudence to make Spinks look the relative novice that he was, with his inexperience being exposed by a ringmaster.

Ali took the first round to find his range, missing wildly and misleading Spinks into thinking he was in for an easy night. From the second round Ali completely bossed the fight, left-stabbing Spinks into disarray and then hooking off the jab and following up with crisp rather than concussive right crosses.

It was 14 years since the then Cassius Clay had 'shook up the world' by taking the world championship from 'big, bad' Sonny Liston. Now here he was on his toes, floatin' and stingin' and taking the young ex-Marine Spinks apart a round at a time. Leon had weighed in at an all-time heaviest 201lb, an indication that he had not trained as hard as for the first fight.

Even when the referee had taken the fifth round away from Ali because he judged that his holding amounted to fouling rather than fooling, the veteran challenger was still comfortably in control against a confused and demoralised opponent.

Spinks tried to rally in the last third of the fight and had his best moments, but he still found Ali elusive as he wrapped up his convincing victory by picking off his desperate, oncoming opponent with deadly accurate counter punches.

There could only be one winner at the final bell and the cheers of the world record indoor crowd nearly lifted the roof as Ali was hailed as the 'new' champion for the historic third time. Referee Lucien Joubert and judge Ernest Cojo gave ten rounds to Ali and four to Spinks, with one even, while the the other judge, Herman Duitreix, scored it 11-4 to the rejuvenated Ali.

ALI AFTER-FIGHT QUOTE, 'Leon is a real gentleman and I'm sure he will get the title back one day when I'm retired and doing all the things I need to do to help the needy of our world. But I'm not goin' to rush into a decision on my future. The title is too hard to get. I'm not going to give it up without thinking things through. I'm going to sit down for six or eight months and think about it. Then I'll decide whether to fight again.

'I've always planned to be the first black man to retire undefeated, and to do it now after being champion three times would be something no one could ever equal. I have made suckers out of all of you. I was training three months before you knew it, and I knew I was in my best shape for a long, long time. I wanted to be good and ready to make history. Now here I am the first ever three-time world heavyweight champion.'

EYEWITNESS – LEON SPINKS, 'My body was ready, but my mind wasn't on the fight. Maybe it was because I had a lot of other things concerning me, a lot of problems that come with the heavyweight championship. Who knows, I don't. That just wasn't me in there, period. But I won't cry because I've lost once, it won't keep me from sleeping or from going back to the gym. My congratulations to Ali. He remains my idol…but I will get that title back.'

WHATEVER HAPPENED TO LEON SPINKS? The lights went out for Neon Leon when he was blasted to a one-round defeat by Gerrie Coetzee in his next fight in Monte Carlo in 1979. He had one more crack at the world title, with Larry Holmes dismantling him in three rounds in 1981. From then on Spinks campaigned mostly in the cruiserweight division. Two years later he had the satisfaction of seeing his brother Michael take the heavyweight crown from Holmes, making them the first brothers to hold the title before the Klitschkos came along.

Leon boxed on until 1994, retiring at the age of 42 after 46 fights, 26 wins (14 inside the distance), 17 defeats and three draws. He briefly flirted with wrestling before retiring to Nebraska and supporting his son, Cory, who became world welterweight champion in 2006.

LEON SPINKS

Leon went through his fortune as quickly as he arrived as champion, getting involved in drink and drugs, two divorces and finishing up working at a McDonald's and as a cleaner at a YMCA hostel. At one stage he was living in a shelter for the homeless. He insists he was defrauded of most of his money by 'advisers', and claims he did not see a penny of the $3.7m he was due for defending his title against Ali. It's been a hard luck story for Leon since he lost the return with Ali, but he insists he is happier out of the spotlight, being looked after by his loving third wife, Brenda. In his later years he has been showing the worrying signs of dementia pugilistica.

Larry Holmes (USA)

Venue: Caesars Palace, Las Vegas
2 October 1980
Ali 217lb, Holmes 211lb
Ali LRET10
(Ali purse: $8m)

THIS was the fight that should never have been allowed, and the fact that it went ahead should trouble the conscience of many who turned a blind eye to sense and compassion. Those of us who loved Ali breathed a sigh of relief when he announced in September 1979 that he was hanging up his gloves, but then we became desperately concerned when a year later he announced he was making a comeback to try to become a FOUR-time champion by challenging Larry Holmes for the WBC title.

This was madness because Ali was already showing the early signs of the Parkinson's Disease that was to reduce him to a shell of the man who had become a legend not only of his sport but as one of the most famous and feted of people in any walk of life.

Three months before the fight, Ali was ordered by the Nevada Athletic Commission to undergo a neurological examination at the Mayo Clinic. The results were kept secret at the time but it has subsequently been claimed that they showed Ali was 'a little off' when he tried to touch his finger to his nose and struggled in several other simple tests. He had trouble coordinating his speech, and in a mobility exercise he had balance problems while hopping on one foot.

Yet despite these worrying results, the commission approved the fight because it feared a huge legal suit if it tried to stop Ali from getting back into the ring.

The promoters constructed a temporary arena in a parking lot at Caesars Palace in Las Vegas. They might as well have erected a scaffold.

Unbeaten Holmes, a confessed Ali admirer and his former sparring partner, was 31 and in his prime, and on a run of 35 straight victories. Grown men sitting at the ringside had tears in their eyes as Holmes dominated the fight from the first bell against an Ali who shuffled around the ring like an old man. This was an Ali shuffle none of us ever wanted to witness.

There were no knockdowns, mainly because it was clear Holmes was showing mercy to his old hero, who was fighting on heart and pride alone. All three judges gave the champion every round as Ali took sustained punishment from the feared Holmes jabs that poured through his defence without answer. At one stage in the ninth round Ali whelped with pain as a corkscrewing right hand punch landed near his kidneys.

At the end of ten one-sided rounds trainer Angelo Dundee decided Ali had taken enough. There was the undignified spectacle of Dundee arguing with Ali's cheerleader Bundini Brown who, with tears pouring down his cheeks, begged for Ali to be allowed to fight on. But Dundee insisted, 'I'm in charge here and I'm stopping the fight.'

Sylvester Stallone, who would not have sunk this low for a storyline for his *Rocky* films, summed it up when he said in a ringside interview, 'This was like watching an autopsy on a man who's still alive.'

ALI AFTER-FIGHT QUOTE, 'I lost too much weight too quickly and it weakened me. Went from 253lb to 217 by taking thyroid pills.

That's what beat me. I felt tired after just one round. That was not the real Muhammad Ali in there. Don't write me off. You wrote me off after Frazier, you wrote me off after Norton, you wrote me off after Spinks, you wrote me off after the draft. I always prove you wrong. I shall return.'

EYEWITNESS – LARRY HOLMES, 'I beat up my hero and I didn't enjoy it. I'm not going to claim that I was holding back, because that would be disrespectful. Once the first bell rang I didn't know who I was fighting. I just got on and did my job regardless of who was in front of me. It's not for me to say what Ali should do now. But sometimes you just have to say enough's enough. He has been great for boxing. He'll always be The Greatest. I love the guy.'

WHATEVER HAPPENED TO LARRY HOLMES? He went on to record 48 successive victories, and was one short of matching Rocky Marciano's all-time record of 49-0 when he lost to Michael Spinks in 1985. Holmes retired after losing a rematch to Spinks, but made repeated comebacks and was unsuccessful in three further attempts to regain the title, including a devastating fourth-round knockout defeat by Mike Tyson. He had his last fight in 2002 (a points victory over Eric 'Butterbean' Esch), ending with a career record of 69 wins (49 inside the distance), and six defeats.

He invested his money wisely and set up a range of businesses in his home town of Easton, employing more than 200 people. In 2014, Larry sold his business interests in Easton, where he remains a huge hero with the main thoroughfare called Larry Holmes Drive. He became a co-host on a TV chat show but still never managed to escape Ali's shadow.

Trevor Berbick (Jamaica)

Venue: Nassau, Bahamas
11 December 1981
Ali 236lb, Berbick 218lb
Ali LPTS10
(Ali purse: $1.2m)

THERE was a desperately sad and unsavoury end to Ali's long and winding road. It was played out in the unlikely setting of the millionaires' playground of Nassau in the tax haven of the Bahamas. 'A Drama in Bahama' the publicists called it, not realising that most of the drama would be outside the ring before a punch had been thrown in the fight featuring useful but limited American-based Jamaican Trevor Berbick.

Right up until the fighters climbed into the ring, Berbick was threatening to pull out unless he was paid up front by promoters who were looking at a huge financial loss. No boxing commission in the United States would allow a licence for Ali to fight because it was so obvious that he was medically unfit. It was heartbreaking in the pre-fight press conferences to hear him slurring his speech and sparring in what seemed a laborious parody of the man who used to float like a butterfly and was now heavy-footed like a buffalo.

Asked why he was continuing to fight despite most people pleading for him to retire, Ali told the press, 'Not because I'm broke. Not because I miss the limelight. Not because anybody makes me. It's just the idea. Four times a champ. I remember when Floyd Patterson regained his championship. Everybody said it was amazing that a man won the heavyweight title back. Patterson won the title two times, but I'm going to do it four times, I always prove the doubters wrong.'

While the spotlight was on Ali insisting he could become the first man ever to win the world heavyweight title for a fourth time, there was unscripted violence in a hotel room across town. Don King, the larger-than-life promoter who had been involved in many of Ali's fights, was beaten up and hospitalised after turning up in Nassau to (allegedly) demand a piece of the action.

There was comedy farce to go with the drama before the fight eventually went ahead. Nobody had thought of providing an official timepiece, so a hasty search was made before a stopwatch was found. Then it was discovered there was no bell to signal the start and end of rounds. After a mad scramble a cowbell was rushed to the stadium. For whom the bell tolls.

Ali reached down into his memory to box with some of his old skill until he tired after seven rounds and began to take heavy punishment from his 12-years-younger opponent. The rope-a-dope tactics did not work because Ali did not have the strength to throw counters, and was just intent on blocking the punches coming his way.

It was only Ali's great pride and amazing willpower that kept him standing in the last three painful rounds of his career. Berbick was walking through his token left jabs and hammering away with both fists to clinch a unanimous points decision. Local judge Alonzo Butler scored it 97-94 for Berbick, and Clyde Gray of Canada and Jay Edson of Florida agreed on a 99-94 victory for the Jamaican.

And that was it. Ali's career was over. A huge flame had been extinguished. We would never see his like again.

ALI AFTER-FIGHT QUOTE, 'Father time caught up with me. I knew what I had to do but the old reflexes were not there. I was beaten by a good fighter, but he would not have laid a glove on the old Muhammad Ali. I've now got to give consideration to my future, and this is likely to be the last you see of Muhammad Ali and this time I won't change my mind. I have a lot to do as an evangelist for Islam.'

EYEWITNESS – TREVOR BERBICK, 'Now I want to prove that I can follow Ali as the world champion. He has been my inspiration since I was a schoolboy. There's never been another boxer like him. But his time has gone. Now it's my time, and I want that title. The promoters here tried to wear me down and put so much mental pressure on me that it was harder than the fight. But I got my money, and I got my victory. Now I want another shot at Larry Holmes.'

WHATEVER HAPPENED TO TREVOR BERBICK? Berbick captured a version of the world title by outpointing Pinklon Thomas in 1986 for the WBC belt, but lost it in two rounds in his first defence when caught in a hurricane called Mike Tyson. It was downhill all the way for Berbick, who was imprisoned for sexually assaulting his babysitter, and twice deported from the United States. Back home in Jamaica, he was brutally murdered in 2006, with a nephew given a life sentence. Berbick was 51. His ring record: 61 fights, 49 wins (33 inside the distance), 11 defeats, one draw.

Ali Facts

Born: 17 January 1942

Birthplace: Louisville, Kentucky

Original name: Cassius Marcellus Clay, Jr, named after his father Cassius (Cash) Clay, a shop sign and billboard painter, who was himself given his name in honour of the white 19th century abolitionist and politician of the same name.

Mother: Odessa (Grady) Clay, who was a household domestic.

Early religion: Cassius Sr was a Methodist, but allowed Odessa to bring up both Cassius and his younger brother Rudolph 'Rudy' Clay (later Rahman Ali) in her faith as a Baptist.

Ancestry: He is a descendant of pre-Civil War era slaves in the American South, and is predominantly of African-American descent, with Irish, English, and Italian ancestry.

Marriages: Sonji Roi (August 1964–January 1966, divorced), Kalilah Tolona (Belinda Boyd) (August 1967–January 1977, divorced), Veronica Porche (June 1977–January 1986, divorced), Yolanda (Lonnie) Williams (19 November 1986–present).

Children: with Kalilah: Maryum (1968), Rasheeda and Jamilla (1970), Muhammad Ibo (1972); with Patricia Harvell: Miya (1971); with Aaisha Fletcher: Khalilah (1974); with Veronica: Hana (1976) and Laila (1977); adopted with Yolanda: Assad (1986).

ALI FACTS

Clay/Ali Timeline

1954: Starts boxing after reporting the theft of his bicycle to a policeman called Joe Martin, who persuades him to take his anger out in the gymnasium that he runs in Louisville. In a six-year amateur career, Clay wins 100 of 108 contests, including six Kentucky Golden Gloves championships.

1959: Wins the first of two National Golden Gloves titles as a light-heavyweight and qualifies for the US Olympic team. Graduates from Louisville Central High School.

1960: Wins Olympic gold medal in Rome, clearly outpointing Poland's Zbigniew Pietrzykowski in the final. Turns professional on his return home, signing with a syndicate of Kentucky businessmen. Outpoints Tunney Hunsaker over eight rounds in his professional debut in Louisville on 29 October. Refuses to be trained by Archie Moore and joins the Miami camp of Angelo Dundee.

1964: 25 February; Sonny Liston quits on his stool at the end of six rounds and Clay becomes world heavyweight champion in his 20th fight. Later announces that he has joined the Nation of Islam and that in future he will answer only to the name of Muhammad Ali.

1965: 25 May, wins rematch with Liston on a controversial first-round knockout. His first fight as Muhammad Ali.

1966: Splits with the Louisville Sponsoring Group and his new manager is Herbert Muhammad, a son of Nation of Islam leader, Elijah.

1967: Refuses induction into the US Army as a conscientious objector, saying, 'I ain't got no quarrel with them Vietcong.

They've never called me nigger.' The World Boxing Association strips him of his world title. New York and other states revoke his licence to box. Convicted in federal court of violating Selective Service laws, sentenced to five years in prison, and fined $10,000. He is freed on bail pending an appeal, and the jail sentence is later quashed.

1967–70: Forced out of boxing, he makes a living giving anti-war lectures at colleges and appears on Broadway in the short-lived musical *Buck White*.

1970: 26 October; Stops Jerry Quarry in three rounds in his first professional fight in more than three years.

1971: 8 March; His first defeat, outpointed by Joe Frazier in the 'fight of the century' at Madison Square Garden, New York. Ali and Frazier split a $5m purse.

1971: 28 June; The US Supreme Court reverses Ali's Selective Service violation conviction in a unanimous ruling.

1972: 20 September; Stops Floyd Patterson in seven rounds, retaining the NABF title.

1973: 31 March; Suffers broken jaw when losing the NABF title to Ken Norton on points over 12 rounds.

1973: 10 September; Regains the NABF title with a 12-round points revenge win over Norton.

1974: 28 January; Outpoints Joe Frazier over 12 rounds to retain his NABF title. Both Ali and Frazier fined $5,000 for brawling in a TV studio before the fight.

1974: 30 October; 'The Rumble in the Jungle' in Kinshasa, Zaire (now Democratic Republic of the Congo). Ali uses 'rope-a-dope' tactics to take the world heavyweight title from George Foreman with an eighth-round knockout victory.

1975: Quits the Nation of Islam to practice the more traditional Islamic faith.

1975: 1 October; Wins the 'Thrilla in Manila' against Joe Frazier, who is retired by his corner at the end of 14 brutal rounds.

1978: 15 February; Loses his heavyweight title to Leon Spinks on a split decision over 15 rounds.

1978: 15 September; Becomes world heavyweight champion for a record third time when regaining the title from Spinks with a unanimous 15-round points decision.

1979: 26 June; Announces his retirement from professional boxing.

1980: 2 October; Comes out of retirement for a guaranteed purse of $8m, and is retired after ten punishing rounds in his challenge for the title held by his former sparring partner, Larry Holmes. He is now showing the first signs of Parkinson's Disease.

1981: 11 December; Loses on points over ten rounds to Trevor Berbick in the Bahamas. It is his last fight.

1984: Reveals that he has Parkinson's Disease, a disorder of the central nervous system.

1990: 27 November; Meets with Saddam Hussein in Baghdad, in an attempt to negotiate the release of Americans held hostage in Iraq and Kuwait, and comes home the following week with 14 hostages.

1996: 19 July; Lights the torch at the opening ceremony to the Olympic Games in Atlanta. The world is shocked to see how badly he is affected by Parkinson's.

2000: 23 October; Appointed United Nations Messenger of Peace.

2005: 9 November; Presented with the Presidential Medal of Freedom by President George W. Bush.

2005: 21 November; The Muhammad Ali Center opens in Louisville, Kentucky.

2006: 11 April; Entertainment and licensing firm CKX announces that it is paying Ali $50m in exchange for 80 per cent of whatever it makes selling his name and likeness. They form a company called G.O.A.T., which stands for 'Greatest of All Time'.

2013: October; Despite scare stories that he is 'at death's door', Ali attends a 'Three Days of Greatness' celebration at The Muhammad Ali Center in his hometown of Louisville, Kentucky, where Muhammad Ali Humanitarian Awards are handed out.

2014: Ali admitted to hospital in December suffering from "a severe urinary tract infection". Released in time to celebrate his 73rd birthday at his Arizona home on 17 January 2015.

The Final Round

An assessment by Norman Giller

WHEN I started out writing this book I wanted it to be an anthem of acclaim to the greatest – yes, The Greatest – fighter who ever climbed into the roped square. But the more I researched, probed, explored and analysed his fights the more I became distraught and depressed by the painful and pitiful destinies of not only Ali himself but of so many of his opponents.

It helped to magnify the love-hate relationship I have with boxing. I love the theatre, the drama, the skill, the bravery, the naked violence of the sport. I hate what it does to the health of its combatants, the winners as well as the losers. It weighs heavily on my conscience, yet I keep returning to the ringside like an eyewitness revisiting the scene of the car crash, in the hope of seeing another one.

You need to be in and around the fight game to understand that there is an acceptance of what is almost a beauty in the brutality of the sport, but we who do the observing from the safe side of the ropes do not have to carry beyond the stadium the consequence of the punishment caused by the punches. We go home with thrilling memories, while the pugilists take home the cuts, bruises and the pain.

The evidence is here in the previous pages that Ali and the brave men who fought him suffered life-harming damage to their health and, often, to their dignity, all so that promoters, managers, trainers, TV and broadcasters, reporters and fight fans could feed off their industry and courage. Yes, some of them earned money beyond the dreams of avarice in return for their gladiatorial skills, but what use is wealth when later in life they become lost in a fog of dementia, with no memory of their achievements and, in most cases, parted from their hard-earned cash?

As I write, Ali has outlived 31 of his opponents, most of them dying from causes linked to the effects of taking punches in the ring. Of those still living, more than a dozen are suffering from pugilistic dementia, or to be painfully blunt, punch-drunkenness.

Since being diagnosed with Parkinson's Disease in 1984, there has been a gradual decline in Ali's health. But, with the staunch support of his wife Lonnie, the heavily-medicated former champion has handled his debilitating illness with dignity and courage, and has never felt sorry for himself or offered a critical word against the raw violence of boxing.

I have been in Ali's company several times since his illness, and on each occasion he has stressed that he is not looking for pity and accepts his condition as a challenge. He continues to worship Allah and insists he has no regrets about a boxing career that sensible judges consider went several fights too far.

There is a generation growing up who never had the privilege of seeing Ali in action in the ring and they only know him as famous for being famous, and their image of him is of a shuffling wreck of a man coping as best he can with the ravages of Parkinson's, the one opponent he cannot beat. They should know that at his peak he was one of the most beautifully and perfectly sculptured boxing champions of them all, and – as he kept reminding us – he was not only The Greatest but also The Prettiest. It was always said with tongue in cheek, but you could not deny the truth of his boasts.

Ali first came to prominence in an unfair and unjust world in which too many were judged by the colour of their skin rather than their abilities. He had to overcome huge prejudices in an era when black athletes could be the best in their sport, yet not sit in the front of the bus in some parts of the United States. Ali transcended his sport to become arguably the most famous person in the world. He not only got to the front of the bus, he drove it. But the bitterness of those early days when he could not be served in a whites-only restaurant or drink from certain water fountains never left him.

I vividly recall a quiet, casual conversation we had in his room at the Munich Hilton when I was working as a publicist on his fight against British bulldog Richard Dunn. Ali was as relaxed as I had ever known him, and was popping questions at me about my life and how I'd got into the boxing PR business. For a man who hogged the spotlight when in publicity-seeking mode, he was gracious and respectful in private conversation, and keen to learn and digest any new facts.

'You're like me, y'know,' he said. 'You have to tell lies to get bums on to seats. I have to pretend to hate my opponents, yet there are very few that I have not liked and I always respect their bravery for getting into that loneliest of places, the boxing ring.'

'You must mean some of the nasty things you say about them,' I offered. 'Look at the way you belittled Henry Cooper by calling him a crippled old bum.'

'Listen, when I get into that ring against anybody I'm secretly as scared as hell,' he confided, almost in a whisper. 'Just take Henry for example. He had a left hook that could send an astronaut to the Moon without a rocket. But I had to make him think he was no worry to me at all. So I used the insults as a weapon, demoralising my opponents to make them feel small and inferior. I am frightened when I get into the ring. I want the man in the other corner to feel even more scared.

'Fear is a factor few outside our sport understand. If you can conquer fear, you have the biggest obstacle out of the way. But if you've got a George Foreman, a Smokin' Joe Frazier or a Ken Norton coming at you, man, believe me only a fool would not be scared. And I ain't no fool.'

Islam was and remains the most important thing in Ali's life, a driving force that became an obsession. He never pushed his views on you in private, but once you were talking to him on the record with a microphone and notebook in sight, he would become a preacher of Islamic ideas and ideals. From 1964 through his conversion to orthodox Islam in 1975, his brilliant biographer Thomas Hauser accurately observed that he was the Nation of Islam's most visible and vocal spokesman in America.

Among the policies Ali preached were:

On integration, 'We who follow the teachings of Elijah Muhammad don't want to be forced to integrate. Integration is wrong. We don't want to live with the white man; that's all.'

On intermarriage, 'No intelligent black man or black woman in his or her right black mind wants white boys and white girls coming to their homes to marry their black sons and daughters.'

On the need for a separate black homeland, 'Why don't we get out and build our own nation? White people just don't want their slaves to be free. That's the whole thing. Why not let us go and build ourselves a nation? We want a country. We're 40 million people, but we'll never be free until we own our own land.'

On brotherhood, 'We're not all brothers. You can say we're brothers, but we're not. There's the whites and there's the blacks, and like birds of a feather they flock together. Always been the way. Always will be the way.'

White extremists hated Ali for his controversial views, but we're all shaped by experiences and environment and Ali was black, proud and said it out loud at a time when the Civil Rights Movement in the United States was going full blast. Ali's views split the nation, particularly after his refusal to join the US Army because he 'had no quarrel with them Vietcong. They ain't never called me a nigger.'

Three of my sportswriting idols were among those who came down on Ali, pouring their words on him like boiling vats of oil.

Jim Murray of the *Los Angeles Times* labelled him the 'white man's burden'.

Jimmy Cannon of the *New York Journal-American* called Ali's ties to the Nation of Islam 'the dirtiest in American sports since the Nazis were shouting for Max Schmeling as representative of their vile theories of blood'.

Red Smith described Ali as a 'draft dodger' and wrote in the *New York Herald-Tribune*, 'Squealing over the possibility that the military may call him up, Cassius makes himself as sorry a spectacle as those unwashed punks who picket and demonstrate against the war.'

Ali also found himself on the questioning end of criticism from other black sporting icons.

Tennis legend Arthur Ashe said, 'I never went along with the pronouncements of Elijah Muhammad that the white man was the devil and that blacks should be striving for separate development; a sort of American apartheid. That never made sense to me. It was a racist ideology and I didn't like it.'

Brown Bomber Joe Louis came out punching against the Ali views, 'I've always believed that every man is my brother. Clay will earn the public's hatred because of his connections with the Black Muslims.'

Former heavyweight champion Floyd Patterson, twice humiliated in the ring by Ali, declared, 'I've been told that Clay has every right to follow any religion he chooses and I agree. But, by the same token, I have every right to call the Black Muslims a menace to the United States and a menace to the Negro race. I do not believe God put us here to hate one another. Cassius Clay is disgracing himself and the Negro race.'

The widespread hatred of Ali gradually melted away as his stubborn stand against the war in Vietnam gained huge public support, and his globetrotting, have-gloves-will-travel approach to boxing gave the world heavyweight championship a standing and a distinction that it has long since lost.

In old age and poor health, he is far prouder of what he achieved as a symbol of black pride and as a resistance fighter against the injustices and racism that poisoned much of America than anything he accomplished in the boxing ring.

He stood as a brave beacon of hope for oppressed people around the world when he refused to become a symbol for America's war with Vietnam. While standing up for his convictions, he sacrificed millions in lost boxing purses and commercial earnings.

Muhammad Ali has flaws, and many of his pronouncements have been poisoned with bigotry and reverse racism.

But as a pugilist and a publicist, an entertainer and symbol of defiance in and out of the ring there has been nobody to touch him.

For me, Muhammad Ali will always be The Greatest.

Previous books by Norman Giller

Lane of Dreams (introduced by Jimmy Greaves and Steve Perryman)
Tottenham, The Managing Game Bill Nicholson Revisited
The Glory Glory Game (Spurs Writers' Club) The Golden Double
Jimmy Greaves At Seventy (with Michael Giller and Terry Baker)
Banks of England (with Gordon Banks) Footballing Fifties
The Glory and the Grief (with George Graham)
Banks v Pelé (with Terry Baker)
Football And All That Bobby Moore The Master
The Seventies Revisited (with Kevin Keegan)
The Final Score (with Brian Moore)
ABC of Soccer Sense (with Tommy Docherty)
Billy Wright, A Hero for All Seasons (official biography)
The Rat Race (with Tommy Docherty)
Denis Compton (The Untold Stories)
McFootball, the Scottish Heroes of the English Game
The Book of Rugby Lists (with Gareth Edwards)
The Book of Tennis Lists (with John Newcombe)
The Book of Golf Lists TV Quiz Trivia Sports Quiz Trivia
Know What I Mean (with Frank Bruno)
Eye of the Tiger (with Frank Bruno)
From Zero to Hero (with Frank Bruno)
The Judge Book of Sports Answers
Watt's My Name (with Jim Watt)
My Most Memorable Fights (with Henry Cooper)
How to Box (with Henry Cooper)
Henry Cooper's 100 Greatest Boxers
Henry Cooper A Hero for All Time
Mike Tyson Biography
Mike Tyson, the Release of Power (with Reg Gutteridge)

Crown of Thorns, the World Heavyweight Title (with Neil Duncanson)
Fighting for Peace (Barry McGuigan biography, with Peter Batt)
World's Greatest Cricket Matches/World's Greatest Football Matches
Golden Heroes (with Dennis Signy) The Judge (1,001 Q&A)
The Great Football IQ Quiz Book (The Judge of The Sun)
The Marathon Kings The Golden Milers (with Sir Roger Bannister)
Olympic Heroes (with Brendan Foster)
Olympics Handbook 1980 Olympics Handbook 1984
Book of Cricket Lists (with Tom Graveney)
Top Ten Cricket Book (with Tom Graveney)
Cricket Heroes (with Eric Morecambe) Big Fight Quiz Book
TVIQ Puzzle Book Lucky the Fox (with Barbara Wright)
Gloria Hunniford's TV Challenge
Chopper's Chelsea (with Ron Harris)
Hammers '80 (with Sir Trevor Brooking)
Concorde Club (First 50 years) Keys to Paradise (with Jeni Robbins)

Children's books:
The Tales of Uncle Rhymo Duncan, the Talking Football

Comedy novels:
Carry On Doctor Carry On England Carry On Loving
Carry On Up the Khyber Carry On Abroad Carry On Henry
What A Carry On
Satzenbrau-sponsored Sports Puzzle Book and TV Puzzle Book

A Stolen Life (novel) Mike Baldwin: Mr Heartbreak (novel)
The Bung (novel) The Glory and the Greed (novel)

Books in collaboration with RICKY TOMLINSON
Football My Arse/Celebrities My Arse/Cheers My Arse
Reading My Arse (The Search for the Rock Island Line)

PLUS books in collaboration with JIMMY GREAVES:
This One's On Me The Final (novel) The Ball Game (novel)
The Boss (novel) The Second Half (novel) Let's Be Honest (with Reg
   Gutteridge) Greavsie's Heroes and Entertainers
World Cup History GOALS! Stop the Game, I Want to Get On
Book of Football Lists Taking Sides Sports Quiz Challenge
Sports Quiz Challenge 2 It's A Funny Old Life Saint & Greavsie's 1990
   World Cup Special The Sixties Revisited Don't Shoot the Manager
   Funny Old Games (with the Saint) Greavsie's Greatest